# Praise for *All Business Is Personal*

"Joseph Michelli's *All Business Is Personal* reminds us that human connection lies at the heart of transformative experiences, whether we're leading in hospitality or healthcare. Drawing on real-world insights from One Medical, Michelli shows how organizations can create environments that support both customers and employees in deeply meaningful ways."

—Chip Conley, Founder & Executive Chairman, Modern Elder Academy (MEA); Founder, Joie De Vivre Hospitality; former Head of Global Hospitality and Strategy, Airbnb; and Author, *PEAK*

"Joseph Michelli demonstrates that the true measure of any business lies in the value it creates for its customers. *All Business Is Personal* offers a vivid blueprint for how One Medical aligns its people, processes, and technology to not only meet customer needs but to enhance their lives in ways that fuel sustainable growth. Leaders across industries will find powerful lessons here on building enduring customer value and loyalty."

—Rob Markey, Creator, Net Promoter System; Coauthor, *The Ultimate Question 2.0*; and Senior Lecturer, Harvard Business School

"Joseph Michelli offers a compelling look at how organizations can care for their customers and people. In *All Business Is Personal*, he highlights how One Medical has created a culture of compassion and innovation that mirrors the employee empowerment we championed at The Ritz-Carlton and continue to champion at the Capella Hotel Group. The lessons in this book are invaluable for leaders committed to cultivating a customer experience culture that supports team members as they deliver exceptional care."

—Hervé J. L. Humler, Chairman, Capella Hotel Group, and Chairman Emeritus, The Ritz Carlton, St Regis, and BVLGARI

"I've been enamored with One Medical for quite a while, as it hits all my hot buttons: human-centered, customized offerings, membership fees, transformative patient experiences, and better outcomes. Joseph Michelli's *All Business Is Personal* demonstrates the impact these ideas have on customers and employees and shows you how to embrace them in your own business. Read this book, follow its principles, and create more valuable offerings."

—B. Joseph Pine II, Coauthor, *The Experience Economy*

"*All Business Is Personal* showcases how organizations like One Medical transform healthcare by putting people first while harnessing the power of technology to drive sustainable success. This is a must-read if you want your organization to reach the highest level of customer or patient delight while at the same time creating an amazingly successful business."

—David Feinberg, MD, Chairman, Cerner Health; former Vice President, Google Health; former President and CEO; and Geisinger, former President and CEO, UCLA Health Systems

"Joseph Michelli understands what it takes to build a company that genuinely cares for its customers and employees. *All Business Is Personal* offers unique perspectives and practical tools like those I've successfully used to elevate experiences at companies like Lands' End and Allstate. Joseph's insights are perfect for anyone who wants to leave a positively memorable impact on those they serve."
—Jeanne Bliss, Author, Chief Customer Officer 2.0 and Cofounder, Customer Experience Professionals Association (CXPA.org)

"*All Business Is Personal* perfectly captures what it takes to build a people-first organization. Joseph Michelli provides actionable strategies for leaders to blend technology with genuine human service, a philosophy key to Starbucks' global success.
—Howard Behar, former President, Starbucks Coffee Company North America & Starbucks Coffee International, and Author, *It's Not About the Coffee*

"*All Business is Personal* flips the script on innovation—proving that in a world driven by technology, it's the human touch that truly disrupts. A must-read!"
—Martin Lindstrom, *New York Times* Best Selling Author, *Buyology* and *The Ministry of Common Sense*

"'Don't read this book unless you are willing to challenge the status quo.' This, Joseph Michelli's opening statement in *All Business Is Personal*, sets the tone for a master class in fusing technology with human connection. As someone who has worked at the intersection of service excellence and leadership, I found *All Business Is Personal* to be a goldmine of insights. The crisp summaries Joseph sprinkles in via his winning through people and technology and quick checkup segments reveal his ability to adroitly condense knowledge into a recipe for action. Drawing on his deep expertise, Joseph offers invaluable lessons on how leaders can transform organizational culture and customer experiences by keeping people at the heart of innovation, much like the Disney principles I hold dear."
—Doug Lipp, former Head of Disney University Training Team, Walt Disney Studios; Speaker; and Author, *Disney U*

"Having closely observed Nordstrom's customer-obsessed culture for more than three decades, I have had a front-row seat to the power of elevating employee and customer experiences. In *All Business Is Personal*, Joseph Michelli expertly shows how One Medical blends empathy and innovation to create customer engagement and loyalty. Whether a mom-and-pop butcher shop like my parents owned or a global brand like Nordstrom, *all* business is personal!"
—Robert Spector, Bestselling Author, *The Nordstrom Way*

"In healthcare, how technology and the human touch are combined determines patients' experiences and profoundly impacts the outcomes delivered. Through *All Business is Personal*, Michelli has once again taken an incredibly complex and challenging topic, increased the difficulty level by applying it to healthcare, and given us a highly actionable road map to success."
—Randy Pritchard, CEO, Axena Health; former CEO, Pillar Biosciences; and former Senior Vice President of Marketing, Roche Diagnostics

# All Business Is Personal

## Also by Joseph A. Michelli

# All Business Is Personal

One Medical's
Human-Centered,
Technology-Powered Approach
to Customer Engagement

Joseph A. Michelli

Matt Holt Books
An Imprint of BenBella Books, Inc.
Dallas, TX

*All Business Is Personal* copyright © 2025 by Joseph A. Michelli

This book was prepared with the assistance of One Medical.

Matt Holt is an imprint of BenBella Books, Inc.
8080 N. Central Expressway
Suite 1700
Dallas, TX 75206
benbellabooks.com
Send feedback to feedback@benbellabooks.com

*BenBella* and *Matt Holt* are federally registered trademarks.

Printed in the United States of America
10 9 8 7 6 5 4 3 2 1

Library of Congress Control Number: 2024054639
ISBN 9781637746769 (hardcover)
ISBN 9781637746776 (electronic)

Copyediting by Scott Calamar
Proofreading by Marissa Wold Uhrina and Natalie Roth
Text design and composition by PerfecType, Nashville, TN
Cover design by Brigid Pearson
Printed by Lake Book Manufacturing

Special discounts for bulk sales are available. Please contact bulkorders@benbellabooks.com.

*This book is dedicated to my grandchildren. May they and their peers inherit and nurture a world where technology assists but humanity prevails.*

# CONTENTS

# FOREWORD

Throughout my career in healthcare leadership, I have studied, visited, and admired great consumer-oriented organizations. I always wondered why healthcare organizations weren't "delighting" people in ways similar to the world's best service companies. I aspired to do so in the healthcare organizations in which I was privileged to serve. One of the key experts I turned to for insights throughout the years was Joseph Michelli, a consultant to and writer of numerous books on some of the world's most beloved brands. When I got to know Joseph and learned about his early professional background working in healthcare, I saw I was engaging not just with an astute management expert but also with someone who understood care and compassion. In Joseph's book *All Business Is Personal*, he turns his eye to describing how One Medical has managed to scale "delight" in healthcare delivery while providing dramatically better outcomes for multiple key stakeholders.

I first met Joseph at UCLA Health, where I served as COO and Dr. David Feinberg served as CEO. As we worked to take UCLA's patient experience scores from the bottom quartile to the 99th percentile in the nation, we engaged Joseph to share insights from many of the other service organizations he had studied. When Joseph profiled our efforts at UCLA Health in his book *Prescription for Excellence*, we learned as much from his inquiries as he might have gleaned from his observations. I took these lessons with me later as CEO at Stanford University's health system, as EVP at

Optum/UnitedHealth Group, as CEO at One Medical, and now as CEO at Healthier Capital.

Building upon the vision of One Medical founder Dr. Tom Lee, the team at One Medical has made positive impacts on transforming healthcare to delight key stakeholders. For consumers, One Medical delivers patient satisfaction Net Promotor Scores of 90 across digital health modalities and hundreds of in-person locations in many markets nationwide while retaining over 90% of its consumer members. For employers and payers, One Medical supports easy employee and dependent access to care in minutes digitally and often the same day in person, all while reducing the total cost of care for payers. For clinicians and employees, One Medical's technology has been shown to automate more than half the tasks clinicians otherwise might typically handle, while One Medical's people experience has promoted a distinct culture of engagement, inclusion, and collaboration. With health network partners, One Medical has digitally and clinically integrated care across multiple settings to better facilitate seamless care coordination and to further own the complexity of navigating healthcare.

In *All Business Is Personal*, Joseph Michelli describes One Medical's approaches for strategically aligning the organization and deploying its activities, for continuously improving processes and innovating technology, and for actively managing performance. He delves into key leadership practices as well as culture and people development activities, while also describing how technology facilitates organizational transformation. He also describes how One Medical leverages the C-I-CARE experience philosophy to embed the customer's needs in all aspects of the organization. Moreover, Joseph describes the positive impacts that One Medical can make on healthcare as part of Amazon, with its aligned obsession for customers, operational capabilities, and technology innovation.

Finally, Joseph captures the spirit of compassion and perseverance of the incredible humans working in healthcare and at One Medical. At the heart of One Medical is the passion to delight, and Joseph has gleaned key insights that have supported One Medical's ability to be recognized among the very best service organizations.

Even as I have gone on to launch Healthier Capital, our healthcare-technology venture capital firm leverages techniques described in *All Business Is Personal*. Beginning with strategic alignment around Healthier Capital's mission to deliver healthier outcomes for all, our team aligns performance through the Healthier Operating System (HOPS) and delights key stakeholders with the C-I-CARE customer experience philosophy—adopting One Medical approaches that Joseph describes herein.

I hope readers will find similar insights from Joseph Michelli's latest book so that they can further delight stakeholders through their organizations.

Amir Dan Rubin
CEO & Founding Managing Partner
Healthier Capital
Menlo Park, California

## CHAPTER 1

# From Start-Up to Amazon's Four-Billion-Dollar Buy

> If you want something new, you have
> to stop doing something old.
>
> *Peter F. Drucker, business consultant*[1]

## DON'T READ THIS BOOK UNLESS YOU ARE WILLING TO:

- challenge the status quo;
- increase the value you provide to colleagues, customers, and business partners;
- more effectively blend human service delivery with technology; and
- learn from a healthcare/technology start-up that garnered the attention of and was acquired by Amazon.

Since you are still reading, I suspect you (like most people in business today) are looking for ideas to address the technology and service challenges faced by leaders, managers, and individual contributors. This book is designed to offer insights on how to effectively blend the powerful benefits of a rapidly changing technology landscape with people's unique talents.

Before the pandemic, many organizations were journeying toward digital transformation (a digital-first approach to all business elements—e.g., customer experiences, operations, product development, and business models). However, mandatory COVID-19 lockdowns accelerated the urgency and speed of technology deployment. The rise of AI, substantial labor shortages, rampant inflation, and increased customer acceptance of self-help options like chatbots have reinforced the critical importance of digital-first, customer-driven solutions across for-profit businesses, non-profit organizations, and government services.

From the perspective of the government, President Joe Biden signed an executive order in December 2021 designed to use technology to improve customer experience and service delivery for the American people. Clare Martorana, Federal Chief Information Officer, and Mina Hsiang, US Digital Service Administrator, described that order as directing federal agencies to be *citizen-centric, simple, seamless, accessible*, and *secure*.

> Every interaction between the Government and the public—whether it involves filing taxes or renewing a passport—is an opportunity to deliver the value, service, and efficiency that the public expects and deserves . . . Technology is not the only component of this effort, but it is a critical aspect of powering an outstanding customer experience, which is why we're making strategic changes in how we plan our technological investments across Government by deploying teams of designers, product managers, and engineers to deliver digital solutions.[2]

While "digital transformation" has become a ubiquitous rallying cry, Patrick Forth, Tom Reichert, Romain de Laubier, and Saibal Chakraborty of the Boston Consulting Group note:

> Digital transformations are difficult to execute. And with so much on the line, only 30% of transformations succeed in achieving

their objectives. There are good reasons for this, too. Delivering such fundamental change at scale in large, complex organizations is challenging, especially with short-term pressures . . .

The technology is important, but the people dimension (organization, operating model, processes, and culture) is usually the determining factor. Organizational inertia from deeply rooted behaviors is a big impediment.[3]

Why are only 30% of these critical digital transformation efforts producing their desired results? More importantly, how can YOU be one of the 30% that blends technology and human service delivery successfully? Writing in a 2023 *Harvard Business Review* article, Leah Leachman (Director Analyst in the Gartner Marketing Practice) and Don Scheibenreif (Distinguished VP Analyst in the Gartner IT Leaders Practice) report:

> Clients often ask us how they should structure their functions to deliver better customer experiences (CX), or what technology they should buy. But that is not the complete question . . . the better question . . . is how to organize in a way that delivers a more holistic and compelling digital experience for customers and employees. A compelling CX demands balancing customer empathy with technology to avoid falling into the trap of what we call "engineered insincerity," or using automation to simulate interest in who you are as a human being. Engineered insincerity shows up . . . in . . . a constant flow of emails from a retailer that bears no understanding of your current situation, chatbots that use slang and informal language to make them appear human, and daily text messages that force you to unfollow.[4]

This book will help you achieve digital transformation success by ensuring your customer experience is team based, human centered, and technology powered. It will also offer an exclusive look into a revolutionary brand-transforming experience creation in healthcare. Like most transformation stories, the journey starts with a simple question: *Why?*

# WHY?

*Why is it so hard to get an appointment
with a primary care doctor?*
*Why do patients unnecessarily wait in reception
areas and exam rooms?*
*Why do patients feel rushed while being treated?*
*Why are most doctors' offices dull and unwelcoming?*
*Why are so many healthcare providers burning out?*

Internist Tom X. Lee asked colleagues and healthcare administrators these questions in the late 1990s while serving as an academic clinician at Harvard's Brigham and Women's Hospital. In response, Tom typically heard: "I don't know" or "We've always done it that way."

Frustrated with healthcare dysfunction but lacking a business background to craft and build a scalable solution, Tom supplemented his medical training with an MBA from Stanford University's Graduate School of Business. In 1999, while attending Stanford, Tom and two classmates (Jeff Tangney and Richard Fiedotin) launched the breakthrough medical reference app Epocrates, which became a widely used clinical information tool for healthcare providers. However, Tom's healthcare transformation vision went beyond the app.

> I grew up in Seattle, where great customer experience was the norm. I'd seen how service worked outside of healthcare and didn't understand why it wasn't a priority anywhere in my profession.
>
> Business school helped me understand the economics of running a company and germinated ideas for designing a modern, scalable, hospitality-oriented medical practice.

While Tom had seen small practices provide quality service, he wanted to build something that would have a large-scale impact and endure.

> From day one, I envisioned One Medical growing from a single clinic to hundreds of hospitality-oriented, operationally efficient

practices. In the early days, I researched and tried to understand what led to the success of other hospitality businesses, such as Starbucks, the Ritz-Carlton, and the Union Square Hospitality Group. I then layered those insights into the foundation of One Medical as we began to pressure-test outdated healthcare norms.

Tom was inspired by Stanford Business School professor Irv Gousbeck, who Tom remembers saying "the only way to become an entrpreneur is to jump in." Tom challenged traditional norms by initially setting up One Medical as a micro-practice. Tom adds:

Initially, I was the physician, receptionist, phlebotomist, accountant, and web designer, which provided a great opportunity to question and understand every assumption I had about healthcare and redesign care delivery.

One Medical would be the opportunity to define new norms in primary care. Thanks to financial support from my parents, a lot of bootstrapping, and many nights moonlighting in hospitals, I was able to validate the One Medical concept and ultimately attract investment capital.

Before we discuss early investors in One Medical and why Amazon purchased the company in 2023 for nearly four billion dollars, let's examine what healthcare and non-healthcare industry leaders can learn from Tom's radical changes in primary care starting in the late 2000s.

## A LEARNING LAB FOR HUMAN-CENTERED AND TECHNOLOGY-POWERED CARE

Technology and healthcare must be considered contextually to appreciate Tom Lee's visionary leadership. Regarding technology, One Medical launched in 2007—the same year Steve Jobs introduced the world to the iPhone and a year after Facebook became a global social media platform. People then purchased mobile GPS units for their cars, and USB thumb drives replaced floppy disks.

In the late 2000s, healthcare was dominated by low-deductible medical plans. According to a 2007 Forrester Research report, "Fifty-six percent of major medical plans sold to individuals have a deductible of less than $2,000, with 32% having a deductible of less than $1,000. Of family plans, 44% have a deductible of $2,000 or less."[5] Forrester also reported that for major health coverage, half of individual policyholders paid less than $122, and more than half of family policyholders paid less than $300 monthly. With low deductibles and the choice of providers largely governed by in-network options, Tom described the One Medical launch environment as a time when:

> The worst and best cardiologists cost the same 20-dollar copay. By contrast, we sought to create differential value by reengineering the practice into a welcoming and modern environment where patients could get same-day or next-day visits with high-quality providers. This was primarily accomplished through administrative workflow design and technology.

Once Tom ensured that he could efficiently deliver a transformative patient experience ("modern, high touch," "easily accessible," and "unhurried care"), he began exploring a membership premium to further validate the value proposition. According to Tom:

> If patients were willing to pay a nominal premium for such a service, we thought we would be onto something. In our initial research, we asked a small focus group (including some of my Stanford Graduate School of Business classmates) what they would pay for same-day appointments, more time with a provider, and the ability to email their doctor. Responses ranged from $10 to $300 per year, but most people were probably in the $30 to $50 range. So, we decided to start with an annual membership fee of $39 and sent out postcards to our existing patients, asking them to mail a $39 check for membership. Crazy in hindsight, but there were very few e-commerce options back then. Most patients sent their payment and acknowledged we'd set the right initial price. Over time,

we further tested price elasticity and bumped the annual membership to $59, $99, and ultimately settled in at $149 to $199.

To fully appreciate how One Medical evolved and grew its membership and to preview lessons you might learn from this trendsetting brand, let's imagine you are a current One Medical member seeking care for flu-like symptoms.

Open your member app and choose an in-office, remote, or annual wellness visit. These insurance-billed options allow you to schedule a same-day or next-day appointment from the app or select from other available appointments with your primary care provider or a care team member. There is no need to call a scheduler and waste time coordinating calendars.

If your symptoms are urgent or you need a clinical question answered immediately, you can also select an option to get on-demand care. Assuming you book an in-office appointment, you will enter a warm, inviting, and modern setting, likely near where you work or live.

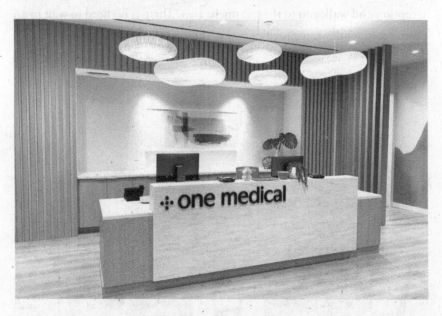

Upon arrival, you will be greeted by a member support specialist (MSS) and seen immediately (98% of appointments begin on time, with an average wait time of three minutes).

Unlike traditional outpatient clinics, your provider will meet you at reception and walk you to the treatment area. There is no need to wait in an exam room while your provider makes their way to you.

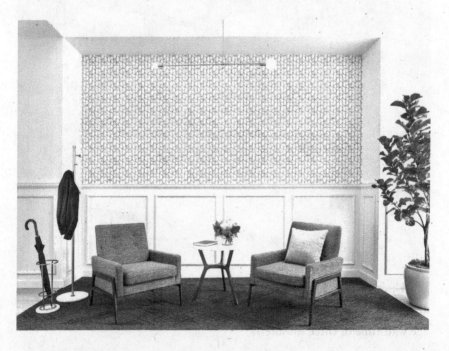

Many traditional symbols that reinforce a power differential between doctor and patient (e.g., a white coat, cues to refer to the provider by their title) are removed to ensure a casual and professional environment that facilitates safety, partnership, and comfort. You have ample time to discuss issues, needs, and concerns in the treatment room.

As a salaried employee, your provider is not preoccupied with rushing you through your visit to get to the next billable patient. A survey by the Physicians Foundation found that typical providers work an average of 51 hours a week.[6] Unlike One Medical clinicians, other providers typically see thirty patients daily, with at least a quarter of their time directed to non-clinical and often tedious documentation tasks. One Medical's investment in developing proprietary software (which produced the user-friendly app you used for scheduling) has also helped your provider spend less time on documentation.

Assuming you need lab work, your provider will guide you across the office to the on-site lab. After completing your labs, you are swiftly and efficiently out the door. Post-visit, your lab results, prescriptions, and a request for feedback on the visit take place through the app.

This is just a quick snapshot of the One Medical member experience. It reflects how businesses succeed when they streamline processes through technology so people are more available to provide service. Later in the book, I will provide insights into leadership and frontline skills needed to design and deliver human-centric and technology-powered solutions that fuel customer experiences. Those insights will have relevance and application beyond healthcare, as evidenced by the attention One Medical has garnered from venture capitalists and business leaders.

## THERE IS NO MISSION WITHOUT MONEY

Thanks to One Medical's high-touch experience, the organization's membership flourished, with Tom Lee opening and operating multiple locations in the San Francisco area. However, Tom intended to scale the business nationally and look for an investment partner who would further accelerate its growth.

> A big unlock for us was the investment made by Benchmark Capital, which funded our series A. At that time, venture capitalist firms were either traditional, healthcare-focused, or fast-paced tech investors (with no appreciation or interest in healthcare services). Benchmark (widely regarded as one of the top tech VCs) decided to take a bet on me and One Medical, ultimately helping create the crossover category "tech-enabled services."

According to Tom, Benchmark's partner, Bruce Dunlevie, was an active early investor who provided guidance and resources for One Medical to succeed. Given Benchmark's well-earned reputation among VCs, their investment in One Medical drew the attention of other investors like the late Jerry Gallagher from Oak Investment Partners. In addition to capital, Jerry brought financial discipline (he is credited with developing the "same-store sales growth" metric) and a focus on four-wall economics. Those elements, combined with Tom Lee's clinical expertise, experience design skills, and hospitality acumen, were crucial ingredients that fueled One Medical's early growth. It also attracted partnerships at academic institutions and medical centers like Stanford and UCSF and investments from companies like the Carlyle Group, DAG Ventures, Redmile Group, J.P. Morgan, Maverick Ventures, and Google Ventures.

From the perspective of Bruce Dunlevie, the Benchmark partner who "took the chance" on One Medical, the decision to invest started with an introduction from Tom Lee's business school classmate, David Kennedy (the founder of a technology company in which Benchmark had previously invested). Even though David didn't expect Benchmark to invest in a primary care delivery platform, he felt Bruce should meet Tom. Bruce explains his willingness to make that connection:

> You have to see 1,000 early-stage businesses to find 10. If you get too judgmental too early, you will limit your aperture and miss something particularly interesting. When I met Tom, he had one unit open in a high-rise in downtown San Francisco—not your typical doctor's office location. Tom was doing everything in his business, and it was evident that he was powerfully intelligent.

Bruce explained that initially, Tom was clear that he wanted to change healthcare, but Tom wasn't sure if he wanted to raise venture capital. Bruce left the door open for follow-up discussions. While waiting for Tom to reengage, Bruce looked at One Medical's limited customer data to understand the attachment customers had to the One Medical service model.

From Bruce's perspective, the annual membership fee made One Medical a promising business. "As a financial analyst, I was impressed with One Medical's adaptation of the subscription model for healthcare. As a result of the financial model, Tom and I spent more time together. I started talking about One Medical as an Amazon-like service business as opposed to a healthcare business since One Medical's customer delight was so high." In addition to One Medical's promising economic model and base of "delighted customers," the company had two additional features Benchmark looks for in investment prospects—a talented and intriguing founder and a unique idea.

Benchmark's first round of investment fueled three more offices in the San Francisco area. Memberships and traffic in those clinics grew quickly through referrals. Bruce notes, "We didn't have to pay for customer acquisition to the degree many customer-facing businesses do. And the renewal rates were extremely high. So, with that success under our belt, we could do a series B investment round. Continued success also led to a series C, and the business grew yearly. It was great working with Tom, and I enjoyed every minute of it."

## BUSINESS-TO-CUSTOMER (B2C) AND BUSINESS-TO-BUSINESS (B2B)

One Medical's membership business (business-to-customer: B2C) was thriving, and leaders had the capital to expand. However, if Tom and his team could attract business-sponsored memberships, One Medical's growth would accelerate exponentially.

Since the 1930s, employers have played a significant role in healthcare consumerism. This employer involvement began with businesses providing company doctors and union-operated clinics for mining, steel production, and railroad workers. The Stabilization Act of 1942 (which limited employers' ability to raise wages) made employer-provided healthcare essential for talent acquisition and employee retention. Writing for *Hub*, David Rook notes, "Because health benefits could be considered part of compensation but did not count as income, workers did not have to pay income tax or payroll taxes on those benefits."[7] With the addition of Medicare and Medicaid, the US healthcare system was essentially funded by employer contributions or government programs.

Since One Medical's revenue model is a hybrid (insurance reimbursement PLUS membership fees), the company's leaders needed to ensure that individuals who purchased a membership would have services covered "under their insurance." This meant One Medical's providers needed to forge partnerships to receive reimbursement under as many insurance plans as possible (more on that later). It would also be optimal if the employer covered the "membership" fee as an employee "wellness" benefit.

Since the 1980s, employers have offered holistic wellness programs focused on increasing occupational health, preventing disease, improving productivity, reducing insurance costs, and managing other work/life issues. If One Medical could show that its transformational model produced value for employees and saved employers' money, the company could grow its membership base through company-purchased subscriptions.

Benchmark's Bruce Dunlevie explains the evolution and importance of One Medical's focus on business-to-business customer acquisition.

David Kennedy, who introduced me to Tom, made a small investment in the first round and was on the One Medical board. He and I had business-to-business (B2B) experience and kept agitating Tom to develop a B2B strategy. Because Tom's first clinic was in an office tower in downtown San Francisco, David suggested that Tom should have a person visit all the offices in the building to see if they wanted access to the greatest healthcare delivery system for not much money. It was an obvious line extension to the direct-to-consumer acquisition path. B2B client acquisition was piecemeal for the first couple of years. Still, we created a professional sales organization, and by the time we sold to Amazon, B2B was approximately half of our business. Acquiring customers 1,000 at a time, instead of one at a time, is a powerful way to grow. To acquire new business customers, our sales team relied on the spiraling effect of devout testimonials like "If I had to give up a benefit offering, the One Medical perk would be the last one I would remove because my employees would revolt." We also needed data to show One Medical's impact on the employer.

Through the years, One Medical has garnered data showing that its offerings benefit employees and employers. For example, One Medical members report 43% lower anxiety levels,[8] and 76% say One Medical "improved their opinion of their employer."[9] The CareFirst Patient-Centered Medical Home Program (PCMH) Ranking of Overall Performance Report also showed One Medical members had 41% fewer emergency room visits.[10] In essence, by providing easy access to care, One Medical members are less likely to sit in an ER waiting room to receive costly emergency services (reducing insurance costs to the employer). Given results like this (and many others shared later in the book), One Medical has attracted and retained more than 8,500 organizational clients who sponsor memberships for their team members. These organizations (large, midsized, and small) include Instacart, Lyft, Nasdaq, Georgetown University, and Zendesk.

## SCALING MEANS SELECTING AND EMPOWERING THE RIGHT PEOPLE

Tom Lee set One Medical on a meteoric trajectory with a transformational vision, an attractive financial model, the infusion of venture capital, and a comprehensive business-to-consumer and business-to-business membership acquisition strategy. Now he needed the right team to expand effectively. Tom was constantly sharing his vision for One Medical and looking for people with the talent and passion to make it come to life at scale.

Leia Vetter, One Medical's Vice President of Operations, Growth, and Services, had been a hospital consultant before returning to business school. Leia shares how she became interested in working at One Medical.

> I traveled a lot as a consultant, so for my business school essays, I wrote about wanting to make it easier to get basic, easy walk-in care, where a sinus infection wouldn't require spending hours in an urgent care clinic in a city on the road. During my first year at the University of California, Berkeley, business school, Tom Lee spoke to my healthcare class about his start-up.
>
> At that time, One Medical had two or three offices in the Bay Area, and Tom's vision resonated with me. I contacted him, and he let me participate in various projects, including inventory, scheduling, and One Medical's electronic medical record (EMR) system.

I joined full-time as One Medical's Director of Operations when I graduated.

Leia noted that her initial interest was to address healthcare convenience and access:

> However, Tom also emphasized the importance of delivering a truly remarkable experience and considering patients as people who should receive human-centered care. I was inspired to help deliver a unique, high-touch, high-respect experience where providers authentically care about people. This was especially attractive coming from a consultative role in hospitals, where healthcare was often impersonal.
>
> At that time, our company office was tiny, with just a few conference rooms and cubicles. As more people joined us, I took calls in a server closet.

Tom Lee recruited Christine Morehead, the former Director of People at Virgin America, to manage the HR function. Christine describes what attracted her to a healthcare start-up, noting:

> I had been at Virgin for almost eight years and wasn't looking to go anywhere. I was proud of how the team at Virgin America focused on every customer experience in pursuit of our mission to make flying fun again. It took me months to decide if I was ready to leave Virgin America, but Tom was such a visionary that I couldn't help but get excited about his inspiring vision. If One Medical could improve the primary care experience, people wouldn't put off appointments until they were gravely ill and would build proactive and positive relationships with their providers. Going from an established company to One Medical was a risk, but the potential impact of the mission made it a risk worth taking.

Tom Lee credits leaders like Christine with helping define and shape One Medical's culture while creating processes for selecting and developing talent.

'Christine was a great thought partner. She holistically and intuitively understood what we needed. She aligned with the idea that people are the most important element of One Medical and focused her efforts on people culture and people processes. We were lucky that she joined the team along with many other talented people who are still in leadership today.

Andrew Diamond, MD, is a leader who started with Tom in the early days of One Medical and is another one of those "still in leadership today." As Chief Medical Officer, Andrew has played a vital role in designing and delivering One Medical's human-centered and technology-powered approach. Unlike Christine, who was hired into a leadership position, Andrew's journey exemplifies One Medical's penchant for developing leaders internally. Andrew received his MD and a PhD in immunology and microbiology from the University of Colorado. After his formal education, Andrew thought he would be a medical researcher with a likely continued focus on pancreatic islet cell transplantation—a potential treatment for type 1 diabetes. However, after completing a residency in internal medicine at Stanford, which included a primary care position, Andrew became energized by primary care. "I found myself surrounded by inspiring professionals who loved primary care. I loved the continuity of seeing patients several times a year and guiding them through a wide range of physical and personal challenges."

Despite being in the heart of Silicon Valley, Andrew was somewhat troubled by a lack of technological innovation in primary care. He and his colleagues believed primary care investments would change the trajectory of American healthcare by preventing avoidable diseases and downstream expenses. Accordingly, Andrew started searching for opportunities to integrate technology and innovation into primary care practices. Andrew picks up the story from there:

My residency program director introduced me to Tom Lee, who seemed wildly ambitious, extremely smart, and partly crazy. Tom wanted to change healthcare across the United States, if not worldwide, but as far as I could tell, he only had one nice San Francisco–based clinic with two other doctors, two physician assistants, a couple of staffers, and no technology to speak of. However, Tom assured me he was building the future of primary care and convinced me that I would be a fool not to join him on the journey. So, I started as a staff clinician, and Tom increasingly brought me into administrative, leadership, and creative projects like crafting operational tools, building teams, and advising the software development team. I got to be a part of shaping primary care technology that enhances human capability. That technology creates an outstanding user experience (UX) through thoughtful design.

## ACCELERATED GROWTH

By 2017, Tom Lee had stewarded his start-up from a single office in San Francisco to 60 offices in eight regions, including Boston, Chicago, Los Angeles, New York City, Phoenix, Seattle, and Washington, DC. One Medical had roughly 272,000 members, $177 million in annual revenue, and more than 1,000 companies sponsoring memberships. The company also innovated healthcare access by deploying a 24-hour virtual medical team and email support. Looking to the future of One Medical, Tom moved into an executive chairman role (maintaining strategic leadership and guidance). Simultaneously, he and the One Medical board sought a veteran healthcare leader who could steward the company toward next-level growth.

Tom and the board chose Amir Dan Rubin as One Medical's new CEO. The rationale for that choice is reflected in Amir's selection announcement:

Amir's tremendous skill set, experience, and accomplishments—coupled with a shared passion for One Medical's patient-first philosophy—made him the ideal choice for steering the company into the future. Joining from UnitedHealth Group's Optum division, Amir served as EVP and divisional CEO, overseeing a number of business lines focused on helping to make the health system work better for everyone. Before Optum, Amir served as president and CEO of Stanford Health Care, where he helped raise patient experience and quality scores to the highest levels in the nation, grow a regional network of care settings, and advance digital health and corporate partnerships in the heart of Silicon Valley. Amir also previously served as COO for the UCLA Health System, where he helped significantly advance quality, service, operations, finances, and growth.[11]

I first met Amir in 2011 when I provided experience design consultation for UCLA Health System. I partnered closely with him in 2013 when I wrote the book *Prescription for Excellence: Leadership Lessons for Creating a World-Class Customer Experience from UCLA Health System*. Our paths crossed again in 2018 when Amir hired me to provide consultative services for One Medical.

Given my relationship with Amir and my access to One Medical through the years, this book will detail Amir's profound influence on the company's operational system, customer care model, and growth strategy. For now, let's look at a few highlights of Amir's leadership, such as positioning the company for an initial public offering in January 2020. One Medical's management company, 1Life Healthcare, opened trading on Nasdaq as ONEM with an initial offering of 17,500,000 common stock shares priced at $14.00 per share for gross proceeds of $245 million before underwriting discounts and commission.[12] One Medical started trading at $18 per share and ended the opening day 58% higher at $22.07 per share.

In a 2023 Medium.com article, Yuechen Zhao notes that Amir was selected to foster One Medical's growth by focusing on partnerships (a component I referenced earlier related to ensuring maximum insurance reimbursements) where One Medical contracted with healthcare systems to provide primary care. Yuechen wrote:

One Medical would bring in the members, provide primary care services, and bill for the care using the hospital system's reimbursement agreements with payors. All the billings go to the hospital system. The hospital system gets access to an attractive pool of patients on commercial plans (which typically have high reimbursement rates) . . . One Medical . . . (1) converts lumpy fee-for-service revenue into recurring capitated revenue and (2) amounts to more total revenue than it might have received as an independent primary care provider.[13]

Citing 2020 data, Yuechen described this approach as a winning strategy that produced "a whopping 38% care margin"—a 6% increase since Amir helped drive health network partnerships. This margin growth occurred as member retention rates remained around 90%—which Yuechen characterized as "an incredible number for this type of membership."

While these numbers somewhat declined after One Medical invested in a 2021 all-stock acquisition of Iora Health (a comprehensive care provider for seniors enrolled in Medicare) valued at roughly $2.1 billion, Amir's six years of leadership produced demonstrable growth. One Medical went from 60 offices in eight regions to over 200 in roughly 20 regions. Membership rose more than threefold to roughly 815,000, and enterprise customers increased 8.5 times to more than 8,500. It was now One Medical's turn to be acquired.

## AMAZON, MEET ONE MEDICAL

When I asked Amir for the Amazon acquisition's backstory, he said, "I have to laugh now because all I wanted was to see how we might partner with Amazon to grow our membership. Here we are on the backside of the acquisition, and sure enough, the One Medical membership is an option for Amazon Prime members." While the original intention to reach Amazon may have been for a narrow partnership, One Medical was an attractive acquisition target.

In July 2022, Michelle Davis of Bloomberg reported, 1Life Healthcare Inc., the management company of the One Medical clinics, "is considering options after attracting takeover interest, according to people with knowledge of the matter."[14] A month later, Michelle wrote, "CVS Health Corp was the mystery bidder that tried to buy primary care company One

Medical before Amazon swooped in to acquire it." Amir suggests Amazon was a solid fit for One Medical:

> We both have membership programs (granted, Amazon's is monu-mentally bigger). Both companies combine logistics, customer care delivery, and tech. Most importantly, the teams at Amazon and One Medical are committed to delivering the best possible human experience and making it easy for consumers to get what they need.

Similarly, upon completing the One Medical acquisition in February 2023, Amazon CEO Andy Jassy noted:

> If you fast forward 10 years from now, people are not going to believe how primary care was administered. For decades, you called your doctor, made an appointment three or four weeks out, drove 15–20 minutes to the doctor, parked your car, signed in and waited several minutes in reception, eventually were placed in an exam room, where you waited another 10–15 minutes before the doctor came in, saw you for five to ten minutes and prescribed medicine, and then you drove 20 minutes to the pharmacy to pick it up—and that's if you didn't have to then go see a specialist for additional evaluation, where the process repeated and could take even longer for an appointment . . . Customers want and deserve better, and that's what One Medical has been working and inno-vating on for more than a decade. Together, we believe we can make the healthcare experience easier, faster, more personal, and more convenient for everyone.[15]

A little over a year after the Amazon acquisition, Amir Dan Rubin left One Medical to launch Healthier Capital, a healthcare venture capital com-pany. He has been replaced by Trent Green, One Medical's COO.

Trent has a more than 20-year history in healthcare consulting and leadership, including roles as an Administrative Fellow at the Mayo Clinic; a Partner at the Tiber Group (a privately held healthcare strategy consul-tancy); the Director of Strategy Practice for Navigant Consulting (now

Guidehouse); and, at Legacy Health, the President of the Legacy Medical Group; the President of Emanuel Medical Center and Unity Center for Behavioral Health; and the Senior Vice President and Chief Operating Officer. In 2024, *Time* magazine named Trent to the Time100 Health list—honoring healthcare's most influential leaders. As part of the selection, *Time*'s health correspondent, Jamie Ducharme, notes:

> During the decade Trent Green spent as an executive at Legacy Health, he saw firsthand how often primary care was undervalued . . . Green, who took over as CEO shortly after One Medical was acquired by Amazon for $4 billion last year, says his next priority is further integrating the two companies, such as by combining One Medical's primary care with Amazon's low-cost, fast-delivery online pharmacy service.[16]

You will read more about Trent's role in integrating One Medical with Amazon in chapter 7, but for now, let's pivot from One Medical's start-up/acquisition journey and explore what you can learn from the company's strategy and leadership.

## GETTING THE MOST FROM THIS BOOK

Before diving into One Medical's lessons, let's preview the book's layout and explore how to use it for your maximum benefit. *All Business Is Personal* consists of eight chapters:

- This chapter introduced you to One Medical.
- Six content chapters cover three change drivers (people, design/execution, and growth) that foster innovation and sustainability.
- A summary chapter helps you take human-centered and technology-powered action.

Structurally, content chapters include "Quick Checkup" questions to guide your human-centric/technology-powered journey and "Winning Through People & Technology" sections for more extensive reflection, discussion, and application of lessons. Each content chapter ends with a summary of takeaways presented as "Transformational Lessons."

*All Business Is Personal* results from more than seventy interviews with One Medical and Amazon leaders, managers, and frontline service providers. It incorporates stories from and conversations with countless patients/members. Pseudonyms are used to protect the privacy of patients. I have also included insights from my work as a human experience consultant with One Medical's leadership team and my journey as a One Medical member.

This book provides tools for organizational and personal growth. In addition to reading it individually, I hope you will consider sharing *All Business Is Personal* with your team and recommending it to relevant business book clubs.

## IT STARTS WITH "HUMAN"

Given the blistering speed of technological change, it's easy to forget that we are all in the people business. We aren't in business to showcase tech tools. We exist to create value for and have a positive impact on people. To that end and to close this chapter, here's an example of human-centered, technology-powered impact shared by a One Medical member whom I will call David.

David had been a member of One Medical for approximately six months and established a primary care relationship with Patrick Portiz, MD, MPH, and the team at One Medical in West Hollywood, California. When David started experiencing urinary hesitation and chronic pain, he used the One Medical app to make a same-day appointment with Dr. Portiz. Based on a thorough discussion of David's recent symptoms and concerns, Dr. Portiz ordered an MRI of David's brain. Against resistance from the insurance company, Dr. Portiz advocated for the necessity of the procedure, given David's unique clinical presentation.

Based on his judgment and advocacy, Dr. Portiz secured the procedure's approval and expedited David's MRI. Upon receipt of the results, Dr. Portiz quickly shared them with David. He had a golf-ball-sized pineal tumor. David picks up the story from there: "Within 48 hours of the MRI, I was in the office of one of the country's best brain surgeons at Cedars-Sinai Hospital—thanks to Dr. Portiz. That surgeon acknowledged that my tumor was rare and that it would be difficult to remove. Even so, he felt there was a high probability he could take it out successfully. He encouraged me to have the surgery immediately. Given the importance of this decision and the risk involved, I wanted a second opinion before letting someone cut into my brain." Dr. Portiz worked with David's insurance company to approve and expedite a second opinion. David notes, "Unfortunately, the second opinion was the opposite of the first. The second surgeon suggested I avoid surgery for as long as possible. Instead, I should enjoy my remaining years knowing that I would encounter progressive deficits like partial or significant vision loss. Given that input, I needed a third opinion to break the tie."

David's insurance company resoundingly denied the request for a third opinion, so a One Medical team member swiftly submitted an appeal and won approval for a third surgical consult. David notes, "The third opinion supported my need for immediate surgery and recommended I undergo a pre-operative procedure called a bubble test to ensure I didn't have an underlying heart condition that could cause a complication during the surgery. As it turned out, I did have that condition, which meant the brain surgery process had to be altered slightly to avoid the complication risk. Essentially, the third opinion made a huge difference in the success of my surgery. Thanks to being able to schedule and communicate quickly through One Medical's app and the clinical care management of Dr. Portiz and the team, I swiftly navigated the complicated process of approvals, MRIs, and consults—getting from diagnosis to surgery in roughly three weeks." Other than a dent and titanium plates in his skull, David reports no residual effects or cognitive changes after the surgery. He is also a One Medical brand advocate and a living testament to human-centered and technology-powered care.

Isn't it time your customers and your business maximized this approach? Let's dive in!

# People

## CHAPTER 2

# Caring FOR and ABOUT People

The simple act of caring is heroic.

***Edward Albert, actor and activist[1]***

## CARING FOR THE CARE PROVIDER

Most business sectors (including healthcare) have clearly defined service roles. There are providers (doctors, nurses, service professionals) and recipients (patients, customers, guests). However, this type of distinction typically oversimplifies a complex ecosystem involving many stakeholders. This chapter will explore a key stakeholder for all businesses—employees. It will also examine how to select service talent, foster collaboration, enhance employee experience, and develop a world-class human-centric culture.

Whatever the industry, your success requires value creation for everyone involved in service delivery. At One Medical, the service ecosystem includes patients, team members, employees, insurance representatives, employers, government payors, and other health system partners. While this chapter focuses exclusively on creating value for the One Medical team (patient-facing and support staff), chapter 3 will explore value delivery for the other people in One Medical's value chain.

Like many other sectors, primary care in the United States faces a workforce shortage, impacting the overall cost of care, population health, and even mortality. The Purchaser Business Group on Health reports:

> U.S. adults who regularly see a primary care physician have **33% lower health care costs** and **19% lower odds of dying prematurely** than those who see only a specialist. The U.S. could **save $67 billion each year** if everyone used a primary care provider as their principal source of care. Every **$1 increase** in primary care spending **produces $13 in savings**.[2]

Unfortunately, according to the National Association of Community Health Centers, many Americans experience barriers to primary care: "Over 100 million Americans—nearly one-third of the nation—do not have access to a usual source of primary care due to a shortage of providers in their local community."[3] The Association of American Medical Colleges expects provider shortage will increase to 124,000 physicians by 2034—more than a third of those will be primary care providers.[4]

Healthcare staffing shortages, in turn, place heightened demands on existing providers, which leads to burnout. The 2024 Athenahealth Survey found that 92% of physicians regularly experience one or more burnout symptoms. Every week, 63% feel overwhelmed by administrative tasks. Sixty-eight percent report they are rushed and don't have sufficient time with patients. Worse yet, 72% believe their organizations aren't set up to reduce their administrative tasks so that they can focus more on patient care.[5]

In an article for *Fortune*, Sunita Mishra, MD, the chief medical officer for Amazon Health Services (AHS), suggests increased workloads create a vicious cycle, causing significant numbers of providers to leave the profession—further limiting supply. She notes that many primary care doctors spend more time on administrative tasks than face-to-face with patients: "On average, physicians spend nine hours a week filling in documentation for electronic health records (EHRs), forcing many of them to stretch work-days into the evenings. This phenomenon is so common that it's frequently called 'pajama time' as doctors continue working on charts after putting their kids to bed."[6]

According to Dr. Mishra, most primary care providers enter health-care to build trusting, long-term patient relationships. However, they can become disillusioned and overwhelmed when most of their work is transac-tional: "While doctors suck in oceans of valuable data about patients, it can be hard to process and synthesize all of it and craft a personalized treatment protocol in just a 15-minute appointment. I remember seeing 100 patients over a series of excessively short appointments in a single day. That's not sustainable for anyone."

From the beginning, One Medical has viewed the provider experience as paramount to successful patient care. Benchmark partner Bruce Dun-levie observes, "Dr. Tom Lee started One Medical with a commitment to elevate the provider experience. That commitment was reinforced by CEO Amir Dan Rubin's vision to make One Medical the best US employer for general practitioners. Since healthcare requires a specialty human resource model, One Medical has created a differentiated and positive experience that attracts providers and mitigates burnout."

That "differentiated and positive" provider experience is built on four key components:

1. **One Medical's movement away from traditional fee-for-service**—In the traditional fee-for-service model, providers are incentivized to increase short visits and only deliver services for which the provider can optimally charge. This unfulfilling approach drives reactive interactions instead of fostering wellness and purposeful relationships. From the beginning, One Medical's model has been to pay clinical providers a competitive salary—rather than having them chase billable revenue.

   This approach enables clinicians to focus on patient relation-ships that promote health and well-being. An Arizona provider notes One Medical's salaried approach is a "good model of care for patients. It offers the opportunity for providers and staff to truly become involved in a meaningful way. This means that compassionate providers are drawn to the model as a way out of the Fee for Service nightmare that kills the soul and mind of altruistic providers."

**QUICK CHECKUP**

How are you ensuring your performance metrics and incentives aren't "killing the soul and mind" of your employees and colleagues?

2. **One Medical's use of technology to decrease the time providers spend on administrative tasks**—Former CEO Amir Dan Rubin explains:

> We've built out technology that reduces the workflow for providers through natural language processing. That technology reads inbound messages sent via the app and routes them to the clinical or administrative teams. Not only does this reduce desktop medicine (tasks where providers are not directly interacting with patients), it also drives down the service cost to employers and insurance companies. Our virtual medical team (VMT) also helps clinicians keep their workday from encroaching on their personal time.

While we will detail provider-centric technologies in chapter 4, Hemalee Patel, DO (doctor of osteopathic medicine), highlights the importance of One Medical's commitment to rapid technology development. Hemalee, a San Francisco–based provider, worked in academic settings before joining One Medical and was accustomed to organizations being slow and resistant to change. Those prior experiences starkly contrasted the collaborative and value-enhancing focus of colleagues at One Medical. While having a conversation with a One Medical design team colleague, Hemalee shared she had:

> A clunky process that took 15 minutes to pull information from multiple documents so that I could lead a group session on diabetes management. Immediately, the designer asked if he could shadow me, and within three days of his observation, I had a solution that made my workflow as easy as two clicks. His human-centered approach delivered a technology-powered solution that makes it easier for me to care for our members.

These collaborative time-saving solutions are producing quantifiable results at One Medical. Benchmarking against 2023 data reported in the *Journal of the American Medical Informatics Association*, One Medical's providers have 58% fewer tasks thanks to technology-powered solutions.[7]

**QUICK CHECKUP**

How are you leveraging technology to reduce time-consuming and repetitive tasks for your employees and colleagues?

3. **One Medical's team-based approach to care**—To avoid providers having exhausting after-hours administrative tasks or "on-call" duties (what Dr. Mishra previously referred to as "pajama time" work), One Medical has developed a collaborative "approach that incorporates a virtual medical team (VMT) that provides 24/7 support."

Natasha Bhuyan, MD, a Scottsdale-based clinician, notes, "Our VMTs play a key role in removing many tasks from a provider's inbox. Because they handle countless patient requests and provide services like reporting normal lab results to patients, providers can focus on the person in front of them." Alani Gregory,

MD, similarly appreciates the One Medical virtual team. "One Medical's team-based environment makes it easier to maintain my boundaries. If I need to get back to a patient in the evening, I don't have to call them at 7 PM. Instead, I can forward that task to a virtual medical team member who is available 24/7. That around-the-clock team support allows me to set limits, ensuring that I care for myself—so I can more effectively care for others."

> **QUICK CHECKUP**
>
> How are you distributing tasks to reduce burnout risk across your organization?

4. **One Medical's proprietary, streamlined, and integrated health record**—One Medical leaders have invested in an effort-reducing, centralized electronic health record (EHR) system. Those investments ensure seamless patient experiences in a hybrid model (in-office or virtual care) and have the added benefit of attracting clinical providers to One Medical. Sally Ward, Primary Care Physician and Medical Director of Clinical Recruiting, notes:

> Our virtual care team and integrated patient records are our secret sauces. Clinicians want to practice in an environment with wraparound support and aren't interrupted all day by triage and advice calls. They also want an easy way to document their services and know that other team members (virtual providers or colleagues in their office) can refill prescriptions and provide seamless care by sharing the same health record. It is a win for our patients and attractive to our top candidates.

> While work/life balance and reducing burnout risk are essential to healthcare providers, these elements are increasingly critical

across all industries—especially for younger generations of workers. Deloitte's 2023 Gen Z and Millennial Survey (which gathered input from respondents in 44 countries) found:

> Nearly half of Gen Zs (46%) and four in 10 millennials (39%) say they feel stressed all or most of the time, and stress levels are even higher among women, LGBT+ respondents, ethnic minorities, and those with disabilities. In addition to concerns about their personal finances and the welfare of their friends and family, poor work/life balance and heavy workloads contribute to their stress levels. And respondents are struggling to disconnect from work, with 23% of Gen Zs and 30% of millennials saying that they answer work emails outside of normal working hours at least five days a week.[8]

Similarly, Gallup researcher Ed O'Boyle notes:

> Above all, Gen Z and millennials want an employer who cares about their well-being . . . But an organization's stance on employee well-being has long been a major factor in where people want to work and how they feel about their current employer—in fact, it was a top three issue for every generational cohort before COVID-19.[9]

**QUICK CHECKUP**

How well are you and your organization responding to the life balance expectations of your team members?

Given the importance of work/life balance and burnout mitigation efforts, let's spend more time applying lessons from One Medical to ensure you are Winning Through People & Technology.

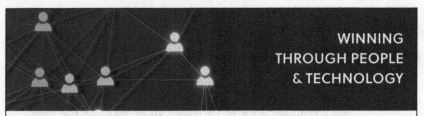

WINNING
THROUGH PEOPLE
& TECHNOLOGY

1. Who are the stakeholders in your service ecosystem?
2. What factors contribute to burnout risk in your organization or
   department?
3. Which, if any, of these three components of burnout are you or your
   colleagues experiencing?
   • Exhaustion or depleted energy
   • Detached, pessimistic, cynical views about work
   • Reduced efficacy or negative self-evaluation of performance
   How pervasive are these types of symptoms in your
   organization or department?
4. What, if any, technologies or team-based approaches have
   decreased burnout or enhanced work/life balance?
5. What technologies or team-based approaches might you, your
   team, or your organization consider to decrease burnout or improve
   work/life balance?

## FROM EASE AND SUPPORT TO CULTURE

Developing "wraparound" support and leveraging collaborative technologies are essential in attracting talented people to One Medical, retaining them, and reducing their burnout risk. However, to navigate One Medical's start-up phase and sustain business success, leaders also had to develop a high-performance service culture anchored to an inspiring purpose and clear guiding principles.

Writing for Foundr.com, Grant Olsen shares global statistics showing that 80% of businesses survive their first year, 50% survive five years or longer, but only 33% survive ten years or longer. Grant cites the absence of a human-centric culture as a primary reason many companies fail:

"Businesses that prioritize profits over people or have a leaders-versus-employees dynamic often fall by the wayside because their toxicity trickles right out of the office and can be sensed by suppliers, partners, and ultimately, customers."[10]

In chapter 1, we looked at Tom Lee's desire to fix a broken healthcare system, challenge the status quo in primary care, and substantially improve patient experiences. We also saw how Tom sought individuals who could help him leverage technology and infuse hospitality throughout the One Medical experience. Leia Vetter, One Medical's VP of Operations, Growth, and Services, expands on this by noting:

> Tom intentionally hired administrative office staff from the service industry, not healthcare. He looked for restaurant servers, hosts, and baristas who talked to people all day, were friendly, and had a service orientation. Once hired, he had them read Danny Meyer's book *Setting the Table* to emphasize the importance of hospitality, and he gave them opportunities to develop clinical skills like phlebotomy. It's no wonder that the people who take blood and give vaccines at One Medical receive the highest customer engagement ratings.

**QUICK CHECKUP**

How effectively are you and your colleagues selecting service talent and ensuring new hires are exposed to hospitality resources?

In addition to looking for service-minded frontline team members, Tom recruited human-centric leaders like Andrew Diamond, MD (the current Chief Medical Officer), and Christine Morehead (the current Chief People Officer) to help him achieve his healthcare transformation mission at scale. Andrew notes:

> Christine was a major change agent for One Medical. Thanks to her, we moved towards a much more professional organization

that was built for scale and growth. As a small company, we were forging culture by having a few people select service talent and getting everyone together for events. However, that would not be sustainable as we grew. So, Tom tasked Christine with defining our culture and keeping it intact at scale.

Immediately, Christine worked with her One Medical leadership team colleagues to refine and continuously tighten the company's mission. It currently reads:

*To transform healthcare for all through a human-centered, technology-powered model, delighting millions of members with better health and care while reducing total costs.*

She also set out to craft a set of core values. According to Christine:

I believe in radical honesty, so I am very open with my team about my missteps. The One Medical Values project was one of my biggest failures. I went through an exercise defining One Medical's values, similar to what we had done at Virgin. I presented the results to Tom, who doesn't mince words, and he hated it. His pushback was that it sounded too much like a marketing slogan and wouldn't resonate with providers. My initial reaction was to ask myself why I left Virgin, but I licked my wounds and took a different approach, which Tom ultimately approved, and we ended up with the DNA as it still exists today. Through that project, I learned a valuable lesson in resilience and think it is important to be vulnerable and share that with others.

Undaunted, Christine and her small team looked to the talented people Tom had recruited (like Andrew Diamond) for purpose-driven commonalities. Christine and her team concluded that the shared qualities of successful One Medical employees were the company's "de facto culture." As such, Christine's team captured those commonalities in five DNA (Distinctive

Nature and Attributes) strands, which Tom readily approved and scheduled for launch at the next company-wide meeting. Christine takes us back to 2014 and the DNA launch—at a meeting in Miami with roughly 350 One Medical attendees:

> The stage went dark, and a team member came out, sat in a chair, and told a compelling story. This was followed by stories from four other team members—a mix of providers, administrative staff, and people with different lengths of employment. The stories ranged from poignant to upbeat but centered around how we care for each other and live our mission. After the five stories were shared, we introduced the DNA, and it was clear the DNA had threaded through those stories, and it is how we work together. We continue to replicate that storytelling exercise by asking cohorts of new hires to share a time they were most proud to work here at One Medical. We do this at check-in 90 days into their employment, which we call One Connection. After sharing those stories, we asked new hires to connect their stories to our DNA strands.

Well before the 90-day check-in, new team members are repeatedly oriented to the One Medical mission and DNA through an engaging onboarding process. As part of an immersive orientation, new hires are methodically and interactively introduced to One Medical's five DNA strands:

**Human-centered**
We stay humble and empathetic, putting people at the heart of everything we build and every decision we make.

**Team-based**
We communicate effectively, respect our teammates, and make the difficult tradeoffs that foster the success of the organization.

**Intellectually curious**
We know we don't know everything; we're always eager to learn, and we're never afraid to question the status quo.

**Unbounded thinking**
By staying open-minded, creative, and positive, we push beyond constraints that have stymied those before us.

**Driven to excel**
In our quest to be the best Primary Care group in the country, we get things done and pay attention to the little details that matter.

Eujin Ahn, One Medical's Director of Talent Management, reports that One Medical's new hire orientation (NHO) "is designed to acclimate new hires to our culture and welcome new team members to the mission, vision, DNA, C-I-CARE, and business overview. The NHO received a 98% favorability score from more than 1,200 participants in 2023. One Medical sends a 30-day survey to NHO attendees, asking them whether they would recommend One Medical as a great place to work. In 2023, 94% of NHO participants responded to that question favorably."

Christine emphasizes that the ultimate goal of continually talking about One Medical's mission and DNA is to have those cultural resources guide behavior and decision-making. For that to happen, the mission and DNA have to be internalized by all team members. Specifically, she notes:

> We want our team members to embrace the culture so much that they use terms from our Mission and DNA and deeply personalize their meaning. They must live their behaviors and not require a laminated card or poster on a conference room wall to aid recall.

Over time, One Medical's DNA threads have been woven into selection, onboarding, professional development, and recognition processes. For example, Sally Ward, MD, reports:

> Our hiring processes have continued to evolve to the point where we were exploring competency-based frameworks. There were a lot of them, and larger companies created their own. Since most frameworks overlapped and we didn't need to reinvent a model, we chose the Korn Ferry framework. We then mapped Korn Ferry's

core competencies to our DNA and refined our interview questions and processes to ensure we captured those aligned elements.
The selection process at One Medical is very organized and team-
based. We look at a prospect's background, skills, and whether they
genuinely want to connect with and serve others in the human-
centered/team-based way outlined in our DNA and competencies.
One Medical isn't a fit for you if you don't work well on a team or
aren't human-centered.

Sally adds that for clinical providers, the One Medical DNA is part
of a review process referred to as "Star Provider" evaluations. This review
occurs at the end of a clinician's third year of employment. Star Provider
evaluations allow the provider and One Medical leaders to assess long-term
fit openly. It is an opportunity to evaluate the degree to which the provider
has demonstrated and embraced clinical excellence, practice sustainability,
and the One Medical philosophy.

**Clinical excellence** involves:
- utilizing an up-to-date and comprehensive set of knowledge and skills
- appropriate use of tests, consultations, and treatments
- forging strong, trusting relationships with patients
- helping patients identify and achieve their health goals
- delivering great clinical outcomes
- communicating clearly and concisely

Clinicians who demonstrate **practice sustainability**:
- employ effective time-management skills
- complete work in a timely manner
- follow through on promises
- display high aptitude with One Medical's technology and systems
- delegate work appropriately across other teams and systems
- build resilience through self-awareness and self-maintenance
- handle challenging situations with poise
- consistently code visits accurately to represent the patient's health
  status and the work done

Star Providers demonstrate the **One Medical philosophy** through:

- dedication to primary care, patients, and colleagues
- a genuine desire to connect with and serve others
- applying a team-based approach to patient care
- embracing and demonstrating cultural sensitivity in colleague and patient interactions
- displaying a sense of ownership in and drive to improve One Medical
- adapting to change and being non-dogmatic
- showing natural curiosity and pushing beyond boundaries
- positively influencing others

Spencer Blackman, MD, who was instrumental in creating Star Provider evaluations, explains the program's growth and importance:

> We have evolved our Star Provider evaluations over the years. Through that evolution, we've always sought to ensure provider assessments were meaningful to the Star candidates as well as the panel evaluating them and that they would strengthen providers' connection with One Medical. We want to continue to recognize providers to whom we would confidently refer our relatives and friends. We want to celebrate their fit with One Medical and invite them to join us for the next phase of their career. The latest iteration of the program expands it past the first round at three years and creates a second round at seven years and a third round at eleven years. It also offers meaningful financial incentives as clinicians successfully move through each evaluation opportunity. In essence, we are celebrating and incentivizing the longevity of those who demonstrate clinical excellence, practice sustainability, and the One Medical philosophy.

While Star evaluations are specific to One Medical providers, core cultural elements are reinforced broadly through corporate events, all-hands meetings, operational activities, regular one-on-one coaching sessions, and training resources (*more on driving operational consistency and individual development in chapters 5 and 6*).

In addition to reinforcing the mission and DNA, individuals are also recognized for embodying the One Medical culture through a series of rituals, including the "fire hose of gratitude." Faith Watson, an office manager who oversees clinics in Tempe and Gilbert, Arizona, notes, "Every month at the start of our operations all-hands meeting, leaders shout out examples of human-centric care, team-based action, intellectual curiosity, unbounded thinking, and a drive to excel. It's amazing how everyone engages in the process. The first time I experienced the fire hose, I had goose bumps, especially when our CEO talked about team-based behavior he observed in one of our labs. It validated why I chose One Medical for my career."

---

**QUICK CHECKUP**

How effectively does your organization incorporate your core values into selection, onboarding, performance evaluation, and recognition?

---

From a new hire's perspective, the One Medical DNA is palpable. When Eujin Ahn, a prospect with an extensive leadership and organizational development background, applied for a position, he was contacted directly by One Medical's Senior Director of Learning and Development. Eujin (now One Medical's Director of Talent Management) notes:

> As I went through the team interviewing process, I felt something was different about One Medical. With my background in organizational development, I was skeptical about the kindness, warmth, and passion for One Medical everyone expressed. Were they selling me on the brand, or was it genuine? As I took the job, I waited for things to change, but they never did. Every person, including the CEO and the Chief People Officer, welcomed me and embodied the DNA. When I went to headquarters (which

we call the clubhouse) for the first time, people gave me hugs. They certainly didn't do that at any of the companies I'd worked for previously.

Similarly, primary care provider Natasha Bhuyan, MD, described her early journey with One Medical this way:

I went into primary care to develop relationships with people and help them on their care journey. So, as I was leaving my residency, I looked for an opportunity that enabled me to develop those types of relationships. Unfortunately, as I started interviewing for jobs, I encountered a lot of positions where primary care physicians needed help managing extreme workloads. In one setting, someone told me she took paid time off to finish her patient notes and tasks. Contrast that to One Medical, where everyone I met seemed happy—they weren't burned out or frenzied. I experienced a human-centered, team-based, continuous improvement culture in every interaction, whether with a Chief Medical Officer, Andrew Diamond, other providers, or administrative team members. I've never regretted my decision since I started here over nine years ago, and I tell people that One Medical is the best career decision I could have ever made.

## QUICK CHECKUP

What do new employees say about your recruitment, hiring, and onboarding process? Do they reference your core values in their description of their experience?

Most employers want to attract and retain employees like Eujin and Natasha—skilled people who fit their culture. They also want to communicate what differentiates them from competitors. In addition to being a place where people possess the five strands of One Medical's DNA, leaders identify their unique points of differentiation as:

A deliberate environment that is fun, creative, and collaborative

A warm setting where everyone feels welcome, heard, and accepted

A genuine communication style, where first names are used more than titles

A focus on teamwork and respect, no matter your position on the team

The understanding that we can all learn from each other, every day

More humane schedules and flexibility to fit your life

One Medical provides a generous benefits program, which includes an employee assistance program that includes free, confidential advice for team members needing help with stress, anxiety, financial planning, and legal issues. The company offers competitive medical, dental, and vision plans, and free One Medical memberships for employees, friends, and family. The company provides twelve weeks of parental leave (paid at 80% of salary) for either parent to care for their new child after birth or adoption and a one-year subscription to UrbanSitter for all One Medical parents. Paid time off (PTO) cash-outs allow team members to convert up to 40 accrued hours per year to cash. One Medical reimburses team members for continuing medical education (CME) and licensure costs.

One Medical also offers a unique benefit—a paid sabbatical after 5, 10, and 15 years of employment. In an article for *Fortune*, Anne Kadet put One Medical's approach to sabbaticals in context, noting:

[One Medical has] given employees with five years of service a month's paid leave since 2013 . . . Not surprisingly, almost everyone eligible takes advantage of the perk, with folks taking time off to herd wild horses across Iceland, teach English in Vietnam, or just stay home to learn a craft . . . While some companies reserve sabbaticals for top executives, One Medical offers the program to everyone from staff doctors to front desk employees. This guards against folks feeling resentful when filling in for a colleague on leave.[11]

> **QUICK CHECKUP**
>
> Are your company benefits aligned with your core values, and do they support your efforts to attract competent, technically talented, and service-minded individuals?

## BUSINESS PERFORMANCE IS LINKED TO CULTURAL DIVERSITY

The "for all" clause in One Medical's mission statement ("*To transform healthcare for all through a human-centered, technology-powered model, delighting millions of members with better health and care while reducing total costs.*") signals two essential elements in the One Medical work culture—diversity and inclusion.

Vijay Eswaran, Executive Chairman of the QI Group of Companies, provided a comprehensive review for the World Economic Forum on the role diversity plays in workplace culture and business performance, noting diversity has benefits to both the business and employees:

> In this era of globalization, diversity in the business environment is about more than gender, race, and ethnicity. It now includes employees with diverse religious and political beliefs, education, socioeconomic backgrounds, sexual orientation, cultures, and even disabilities. Companies are discovering that, by supporting and promoting a diverse and inclusive workplace, they are gaining benefits that go beyond the optics.[12]

Vijay highlights research that shows that diversity is associated with an organization's increased profitability and creativity, enhanced governance, and improved problem-solving.

Diversity is also linked to greater organizational resilience and effectiveness. A study by the Boston Consulting Group found that organizations with above-average diversity on their management teams reported innovation revenue (at 45% of total revenue), 19 percentage points higher than counterparts with below-average leadership diversity (innovation revenue at 26% of total revenue).[13] Similarly, McKinsey & Company has conducted four studies on the role of leadership diversity and business performance. In the McKinsey report published in 2023, Dame Vivian Hunt from United-Health Group, Sundiatu Dixon-Fyle, Celia Huber, María del Mar Martínez Márquez, Sara Prince, and Ashley Thomas from McKinsey note:

> The business case is the strongest it has been since we've been tracking and, for the first time in some areas, equitable representation is in sight. Further, a striking new finding is that leadership diversity is also convincingly associated with holistic growth ambitions, greater social impact, and more satisfied workforces.[14]

The findings of the McKinsey research on workforce satisfaction may reflect a changing view on workplace inclusivity. Millennials, estimated to represent 75% of the modern workforce, value inclusion more than prior generations. In a summary of findings on generational differences concerning the importance of workplace inclusion, Gallup's Global Practice Leader, Ed O'Boyle, notes:

> Younger generations grew up in a world that was far more diverse than previous generations. They demand respect, equity, and inclusion— and they are voting with their consumer and employment choices. Diversity, equity, and inclusion (DEI) is not a "nice to have" for this generation; it's an imperative that is core to their personal identities.[15]

**QUICK CHECKUP**

How diverse is your organization across leadership, management, and frontline team members? How is your level of diversity affecting innovation revenue, social impact, and employee engagement?

Former CEO Amir Dan Rubin indicated that One Medical has *consistently* sought and tracked inclusivity: "In 2021, 72% of our employees and 75% of our providers were women. Roughly 5% of our employees declined to state their ethnicity, but of those that did, 47% of our employees and 37% of our providers identified as people of color. One Medical strives to represent our communities and be a great place for everyone to work."

Alani Gregory, MD, One Medical's Head of Diversity, Inclusion, and Health Equity, speaks to the importance of having team members who "represent the communities they serve."

> People want to be treated by people they identify with and trust. Many people choose me to care for them because they feel most comfortable being seen by a woman or person of color. That comfort makes them more likely to engage in their care, leading to better clinical outcomes.

Dr. Gregory's perspective is supported by longitudinal research like a 2023 study conducted by John E. Snyder, MD, MS, MPH; Rachel D. Upton, PhD; Thomas C. Hassett, PhD; et al., reported in *JAMA Network Open*, which found:

> Higher levels of Black representation within the physician workforce were observed to be directly associated with longer life expectancy and inversely associated with all-cause mortality rates and all-cause mortality rate disparities for Black individuals. Hence, Black representation levels likely have relevance for population health, supporting the need to expand the structural diversity of the health workforce.[16]

At a more personal level, Hemalee Patel, DO (One Medical clinical provider and National Senior Medical Director), shares an example of the benefits patients receive by engaging with One Medical clinicians from diverse backgrounds:

> Being South Asian, I've seen family members go through bouts with diabetes and be told to increase meat intake. However, as

vegetarians, they couldn't make those changes without sacrific-
ing their values and beliefs. By contrast, my team and I recently
helped a pre-diabetic Filipina woman who was afraid she would
have to stop attending family events to keep her blood sugars in
a healthy range. She was delighted to learn how she could make
healthy lifestyle changes without adopting a culturally untenable
diet regimen.

One Medical further supports diversity and community through
employee resource groups (ERGs), committees, training, and mentorship.
ERGs are voluntary, employee-led groups that encourage an environment
where team members "are comfortable bringing their authentic selves to
work." One Medical's ERGs are:

- Asian, Pacific Islander, and Desi-American ERG
- Black Excellence ERG
- Disabled ERG
- Gender Expansive ERG
- Hispanic/Latinx Organization for Leadership and Advancement ERG
- South/West Asian, North African, & Refugee ERG
- Veterans ERG
- Women at One Medical ERG

One Medical's domain working groups, guilds, and committees serve
as knowledge centers on specific topics. Several of these groups are dedicated to diversity, equity, and inclusion, such as:

- Diversity, Equity, Inclusion, and Justice Committee
- Health Equity Domain Working Group
- Tech Diversity, Inclusion, and Belonging Guild
- Tech Accessibility Guild

From a training perspective, One Medical provides a diversity, inclusion, and health equity (DIHE) learning curriculum. These company-
wide trainings create a shared foundation for DIHE and strengthen the

knowledge and skills needed to create a diverse, inclusive, and equitable healthcare experience for employees, leaders, and patients. The training includes modules on workplace diversity, preventing discrimination and microaggressions, and diagnosing unconscious bias.

One Medical's Head of Diversity, Inclusion, and Health Equity, Alani Gregory, MD, notes:

> Additionally, we offer clinician education and are proud of our National Rounds program, which embeds health equity into various primary care topics, often not seen in standard medical education. We also create specific content on caring for historically marginalized populations. For example, topics include dermatology for skin of color, gender-affirming care, trauma-informed care, obesity stigma and treatment, and culturally sensitive communication.

One Medical team members involved in recruitment and hiring also receive additional and ongoing courses related to unconscious bias during the selection process. Dr. Sally Ward, a leader who trains others on selection bias, shares:

> One of the main points of training is that you have to get outside of your comfort zone and recognize bias in yourself. Sometimes, an interviewer will feel a tug of bias that they must pay attention to and work against. An example occurs when you're five minutes into an interview and think, *There's no way I'm going to advance this candidate*, or *I wish they'd speed this up*. When those tugs happen, we must refocus because everybody deserves the same standard process and the same chance to shine.

As it relates to mentorship, One Medical provides many groups and programs. For example, the Black, Indigenous, and People of Color (BIPOC) Mentorship program is "an annual three-month program that invests in and promotes career development for BIPOC team members. Through this program, One Medical seeks to facilitate exposure to different career paths and equip team members with knowledge and tools to navigate their career aspirations." In 2023, this BIPOC program had 148 mentor and mentee pairs, garnering an 88% satisfaction rate and 27 promotions into new roles.

Let's take a moment to apply culture lessons from One Medical to ensure you are Winning Through People & Technology.

WINNING
THROUGH PEOPLE
& TECHNOLOGY

1. On a scale of 1–10 (with 1 being low and 10 being high), how would you rate your organization or department based on "human-centricity"? What is the basis of this rating? What, if anything, would it take to increase that score? What role do you play in elevating your department or organization's human-centricity?

2. To what degree are elements of your culture (mission, vision, values) ingrained into the memory, decision-making, and behaviors of everyone in your organization? Beyond laminated cards and wall signs, how does your department or organization help team members internalize those cultural constructs?

3. Have you linked your core values and mission to core competencies assessed during the selection process? If so, how has that alignment ensured you choose people who fit your culture? If not, how can you assist with incorporating mission and values into selection?

4. Assume someone were to ask you about what makes your workplace unique. What would you tell them? What are the differentiating elements of your employee value proposition?

5. How would you describe your department's diversity, equity, and inclusivity? What are your strengths and opportunities as it relates to DEI? How does your departmental or organizational diversity affect the people and communities you serve?

## EFFORT DOESN'T NECESSARILY PREDICT OUTCOMES

The legendary UCLA basketball coach John Wooden reportedly said, "Don't confuse activity with results."[17] His quote prompts this question for One Medical: Do the leadership efforts outlined throughout this chapter produce a collaborative, inclusive, human-centered culture? From the perspective of employee engagement, team member sentiment, and external recognition, the answer is "YES."

Leaders at One Medical biannually assess overall employee engagement by asking every team member to evaluate their One Medical experience from the perspective of well-being, belonging, management, diversity, enablement, alignment and involvement, teamwork and ownership, and learning and development. Some of the prompts used to assess these engagement drivers include:

- I know how my work contributes to the goals of One Medical. *(Alignment and involvement)*
- I know what I need to do to be successful in my role. *(Alignment and involvement)*
- My manager fosters an inclusive team. *(Belonging)*
- One Medical values diversity. *(Diversity)*
- I can work productively in my current environment. *(Enablement)*
- We have enough autonomy to perform our jobs effectively. *(Enablement)*
- My manager (or someone in management) has shown a genuine interest in my career aspirations. *(Learning and development)*
- My manager keeps me informed about what is happening. *(Management)*
- My manager gives me useful feedback on how well I am performing. *(Management)*
- My manager genuinely cares about my well-being. *(Management)*
- I feel I am part of a team. *(Teamwork and ownership)*
- In general, I feel what I do at work is worthwhile. *(Well-being)*
- I receive support from team members around me at work when I need it. *(Well-being)*

Results of employee engagement in 2023 reflect the highest participation rate in the survey's history (84%). One Medical's overall highly favorable results spotlight exceptional performance in management, alignment, teamwork, and learning, with clinical providers giving the highest rating on well-being (79% favorable) versus the all-company rating (75%). Cherie Woodbury (One Medical's Head of Talent Management) notes:

> Our philosophy is that engagement reflects the emotional connection of our team members to our mission, goals, and objectives. By increasing it, we can positively impact growth, performance, innovation, and retention. Provider engagement and well-being also have a direct impact on patient care. How patients perceive their provider impacts how they participate in and experience their care, which may have many implications on patient satisfaction scores and clinical outcomes.

In addition to high engagement and well-being scores, One Medical has solid retention rates for clinical and non-clinical team members. Attrition rates through October 2023 were 10.2% company-wide, with provider and all-company attrition rates trending lower than in previous years. These results are in contrast to 2024 DailyPay findings for healthcare roles:

- Registered nurses: 18.4%
- Certified nursing assistant (CNA): 41.8%
- Physician assistant (PA): 11.1%
- Physical therapist: 12.1%
- Medical technologist: 15.9%
- Pharmacist: 10.7%
- Radiologic technologist: 15.2%
- Patient care tech (PCT): 36.3%[18]

Christine Morehead, One Medical's Chief People Officer, contextualizes One Medical's use of engagement surveys, noting: "We see the survey process as a way to supplement what we learn from team members through regular conversations like one-on-ones. We also use all team members' feedback to constantly improve the experience for each other. This approach has helped us manage the challenges of delivering healthcare during COVID-19 and navigating natural anxieties during our IPO and the Amazon acquisition."

Cherie Woodbury and her team help leaders evaluate employee engagement data and build action plans. Cherie notes: "We consult with our colleagues to help them understand and look for ways to drive engagement. We ask a lot of questions so they can eliminate issues that detract from an optimal employee experience or increase employee pride and the desire to extend their employment at One Medical."

Over the years, One Medical has earned its share of third-party recognition for its culture, including certification as a Great Place to Work and being named by *Forbes* as one of America's best midsized businesses for three consecutive years (2021–2023). Concerning the *Forbes* recognition, *Forbes* and Statista select America's best employers through an independent survey applied to a sample of approximately 45,000 employees working for American companies and institutions with more than 1,000 employees. The *Forbes* evaluation is based on indirect and direct recommendations from employees who are asked to rate their willingness to recommend their employers to friends and family.

While industry recognition indicates that One Medical's culture is strong, the ultimate validation lives in team members' perceptions. Former Amazon CEO Jeff Bezos said, "Your brand is what people say about you when you're not in the room." One Medical's brand is exemplified by stories shared on websites like Indeed. Some of those comments include the following.

According to an Advanced Task Team Member:

One Medical offers an amazing work environment for like-minded employees who are kind-hearted and motivated to make a difference in the lives of others. They offer amazing benefits and endless advancement opportunities. They truly care about their team members and their families . . . Hands down, it is the best company

I have ever worked for. I have learned so much here and have grown as a professional in the healthcare field. I have learned more at One Medical than I have in any classroom.

A Lab Service Specialist shares:

I had some personal issues when I was just one month in, and One Medical gave me the support that I needed to get through it, all while working. Being Human-Centered is not a slogan, but it is the Way of Life that is presented every day within the company and with those we care for. I've been working at One Medical for two years, and with Blessings, I will be retiring! That was the best decision I made!

A Member Support Specialist notes:

I have worked in the healthcare industry for years in many different roles, and how One Medical operates definitely is not the status quo. My day is focused on ensuring our patients get the necessary authorizations for their procedure orders, consult orders, and medications. I work virtually, helping our patients nationwide. One Medical has provided the necessary tools and training to ensure I feel comfortable in my role. My managers are one of those tools. I can ask for support where needed without fear of backlash. Aside from my role, our team has been building our team culture from the ground up.

Finally, a physician shares:

An amazing group of smart and engaged people who are changing the way healthcare is provided in America. Leadership is thoughtful and mission driven. The company is adapting rapidly to continuously improve. Patients love the model, which puts primary care at the forefront of healthcare.

Caring for team members is a journey, *not* a destination. Caring requires vigilance and a commitment to continuous improvement. If done well, organizations attract diverse people, enhance their talents, and encourage them to collaborate by shared values and a purposeful vision. That success translates into discretionary effort, retention, and positive customer, vendor, and partner outcomes. Before we look at how stakeholders benefit from a well-cared-for team, let's take a moment to look at this chapter's Transformational Lessons.

## TRANSFORMATIONAL LESSONS

- Edward Albert suggests, "The simple act of caring is heroic."
- Whatever your business, success requires value creation for everyone involved in service delivery.
- Businesses fail when they don't create collaborative human-centric cultures.
- Work/life balance and reducing burnout risk are increasingly important across all industries, especially for younger generations of workers.
- Research findings from Deloitte show that "Nearly half of Gen Zs (46%) and four in 10 millennials (39%) say they feel stressed all or most of the time . . ."
- Gallup research shows, "Above all, Gen Z and millennials want an employer who cares about their well-being . . ."

- A company's mission, vision, and values should be clear and actionable.
- When selecting team members, organizations should link cultural elements to desired competencies.
- Onboarding should ensure that team members internalize and can act according to a company's mission, vision, and values.
- Team members should be supported to develop behaviors that align with an organization's mission, vision, and values.
- Workplace diversity is associated with increased profitability and creativity, enhanced governance, and improved problem-solving.
- Gallup's research suggests that younger generations "demand respect, equity, and inclusion—and they are voting with their consumer and employment choices." Diversity, equity, and inclusion (DEI) are not "nice to have" for this generation; they are imperative and core to their identities.
- John Wooden said, "Don't confuse activity with results."
- When it comes to results related to company culture, listen to team members informally and through surveys. Leverage that listening to continuously improve the employee experience.

## CHAPTER 3

# Doing Right by ALL Stakeholders

In an age where everything and everyone is
linked through networks of glass and air, no
one—no business, organization, government
agency, country—is an island. We need to do
right by all our stakeholders . . . no organization
can succeed in a world that is failing.

*Don Tapscott, business executive,*
*author, and consultant[1]*

## VALUE NETWORKS

Who is in your value network? Will Kenton, writing for Investopedia,
defines a value network as:

*A set of connections between organizations and/or*
*individuals interacting with each other to benefit the entire*

57

*group. A value network allows members to buy and sell products as well as share information. These networks can be visualized with a simple mapping tool showing nodes (members) and connectors (relationships).[2]*

Using Will's terminology, chapter 2 focused on the relationship between two nodes—One Medical's leaders and team members. This chapter will look at value creation across other nodes and relationships. Specifically, we will explore One Medical's connection to business clients, the employees of those clients, private and government insurers, healthcare network partners, individual One Medical members, and even patients who aren't part of the One Medical system. This exploration will give you insights into creating value across your service ecosystem while implementing a successful partnership strategy.

As you'll recall from chapter 1, we examined how employers invest in health plans and supplemental wellness benefits (such as One Medical memberships) to attract, retain, and keep their employees healthy. We also previewed high-level data showing that One Medical creates value for employers and employees. Let's take a deeper dive into those findings.

## CARING FOR EMPLOYERS, EMPLOYEES, AND INSURERS

According to the KFF 2023 Health Benefits Survey, almost 153 million (non–Medicare eligible) people receive employer-sponsored health benefits. The average annual premium for employer-sponsored insurance was $8,495 for single and $23,968 for family coverage. Ninety percent of workers with single coverage were required to meet an annual deductible, averaging $1,735, before most services were reimbursed. Among workers with single coverage and a deductible, that deductible increased by 10% since 2018 and 53% since 2013. Since 2018, the average premium for family coverage has increased by 22%.[3]

In addition to affecting employees, rising healthcare costs also affect employers and insurance carriers. In the employer-sponsored health insurance marketplace, employers either self-fund (assume the risk) or purchase coverage from an insurance company that assumes the risk. Self-funded plans are administered by the employer or, more commonly, managed by a third-party administrator (TPA). Those TPAs are typically commercial insurance carriers who *don't* assume risk and instead receive fees for administering the plans that enrollees select.

When providers like One Medical decrease healthcare costs, those reductions benefit the employer (in a self-funding model) or the insurance carrier (in a traditional insurance model). Writing for Axios in the third quarter of 2023, Tina Reed, the author of "Axios Vitals," noted that "employers are facing the most significant annual increase in healthcare costs in a decade, according to Mercer. Two-thirds of the employer health insurance market is in self-insured plans."[4]

Against this backdrop, One Medical serves all stakeholders (employers, insurers, and plan enrollees) by reducing costs without compromising quality. In a seminal paper titled "Utilization and Cost of an Employer-Sponsored Comprehensive Primary Care Delivery Model" published in the *JAMA Network Open*, One Medical's membership-based primary care model demonstrated substantial cost savings. In that study, researchers Sanjay Basu, MD, PhD; Tyler Zhang, BA; Alli Gilmore, PhD; Esha Datta, PhD; and Eun Yeong Kim, BA, asked, "What are the utilization rates and costs of service of a comprehensive primary care model that incorporates employer-sponsored on-site, near-site, and virtual primary care?"[5] Their peer-reviewed study, facilitated by Collective Health (an integrated healthcare solutions provider that administers health plans for businesses), compared roughly 1,980 One Medical members (employees and dependents of an aerospace engineering and manufacturing company) to a matched group of employees from other primary care providers. The researchers descriptively and quantitatively analyzed cost and utilization differences between One Medical's comprehensive delivery model and community-based equivalents. (*Please refer to the Sanjay Basu et al. endnote to learn more about the study's design*).

Here are high-level findings from that study related to utilization rates and costs associated with One Medical's on-site, near-site, and virtual primary care model:

- Members who utilized One Medical had lower overall health spending on a risk-adjusted basis.
- The One Medical approach reproduces increased costs for primary care and mental health services:
  — 109% higher spending on primary care ($20 per member per month—PMPM)
  — 20% higher spending on mental health care ($1 PMPM)
- Savings on costly downstream care, such as emergency care, hospital visits, prescription medications, and radiology, eclipsed those increases:
  — 45% lower total medical and prescription claims costs ($167 PMPM)
  — 54% lower spending on specialty care ($11 PMPM)
  — 43% lower spending on surgery ($14 PMPM)
  — 33% lower spending on emergency department care ($16 PMPM)
  — 26% lower spending on prescriptions ($5 PMPM)

The net result is that *One Medical clients saved 45% in medical costs—roughly $167 per member per month.*

Similarly, an ongoing longitudinal One Medical case study, running since 2015, shows an 8% saving in the total cost of care for the employer. This reflects a 3.5% reduction in medical costs (increased primary care access and decreased ER, urgent care, and specialty visits), a 4% reduction in time costs, and a 0.8% savings from claim-free virtual services.[6]

**QUICK CHECKUP**

How are you reducing costs while maintaining quality for your stakeholders? How can you demonstrate those savings?

# LOWER PRICE AND INCREASE VALUE

Warren Buffett reportedly said, "Price is what you pay. Value is what you get." As such, price reductions are just a part of the value equation for employers offering One Medical benefits. Specifically, One Medical improves employee mental health and enhances employee perceptions of the employer.

The 2022 National Survey on Drug Use and Health, conducted by SAMHSA (Substance Abuse and Mental Health Services Administration), suggests America is facing a substance use and mental health crisis.

- 48.7 million people (17.3% of those over the age of 12) had a substance use disorder (SUD).
- 94.7% with SUD did *not* seek treatment or think they needed care.
- 15.4 million adults (6% of those over the age of 18) had a serious mental illness (SMI).
- 4.8 million adolescents (19.5% of those aged 12 to 17) had a major depressive episode (MDE).
- 22.5 million adults (8.8% of people over 18) had an MDE.[7]

The Anxiety and Depression Association of America reports anxiety disorders (the most common mental illness in America) affect 40 million adults (roughly 19.1% of the population).[8] According to the Centers for Disease Control and Prevention, 49,449 people died by suicide in 2022—the highest rate since 1941.[9]

In short, substance misuse, mental illness, and suicide are traumatizing individuals, families, and businesses. The National Alliance on Mental Illness outlines the cascading effect of mental illness on:

**Individuals:**
- When compared to the general population, people with depression have a 40% increased risk of cardiovascular and metabolic diseases. The risk is nearly 200% greater for individuals with serious mental illness.

**Families:**
- At least 8.4 million Americans provide care to an adult with an emotional or emotional health issue.
- Individuals spend, on average, 32 hours a week caring for adult family members with mental or emotional health issues.

**Businesses:**
- Across the US economy, $193 billion is lost each year due to serious mental illness.
- Globally, depression is the leading cause of disability, and the combination of depression and anxiety disorders results in over a trillion dollars in lost annual productivity.[10]

Given the impact of emotional and mental health issues, One Medical leverages its team, human-centricity, and technology to provide a longitudinal approach that integrates a broad spectrum of mental health services into primary care. That integration, depicted below, leverages virtual and in-person visits across primary care appointments, group therapy, individual therapy, medication consults, medication management, wellness workshops, one-on-one health coaching, and employer wellness resources.

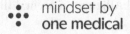

A suite of behavioral health services anchored in exceptional primary care, built for better long-term health outcomes at lower cost.

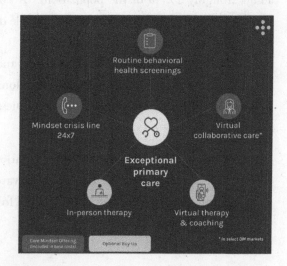

Data compiled by One Medical shows that this comprehensive human-centered, technology-powered approach results in a greater than 50% reduction in severe anxiety when individuals participate in One Medical's group visits and virtual behavioral solutions. Similarly, one-to-one coaching and group therapy provided by One Medical teams show a greater than 50% reduction in Patient Health Questionnaire (PHQ-9) scores (a diagnostic tool that screens for depression). When medication is part of the treatment regime, One Medical providers prescribe generic anti-anxiety medications and antidepressants more than 96% of the time—resulting in additional cost savings for employers and insurers.

In addition to reducing costs and increasing the well-being of employees, One Medical's value proposition for employers includes fostering the relationship between employer and team members. In a study of HR leaders and full-time employees conducted in partnership with the independent research firm Workplace Intelligence, 65% of employees said they would "give up key perks like bonuses, vacation, and flexible hours for better healthcare benefits." That same study found "nearly all (99%) of HR leaders and 87% of employees agreed that providing a healthcare offering that is a good value, high-quality, and patient-centered increases job satisfaction, engagement, retention, recruitment, likelihood to recommend the company, and productivity."[11]

Eighty-five percent of HR leaders reported their companies save money when employees regularly see primary care providers. Similarly, One Medical's member satisfaction data shows that 76% of employees/members had an improved opinion of their employer as a result of their employer providing One Medical as a benefit. Given the challenges of engaging employees, strengthening the relationships between employees and employers is especially important.

In a 2024 Gallup Workplace report, Jim Harter described an 11-year low in employee engagement, noting:

Unfortunately the first quarter of 2024 continued this downward trend, with engagement dropping three percentage points to 30% among both full- and part-time employees. This decline represents

4.8 million fewer employees engaged in their work and work-place, marking the lowest reported level of engagement since 2013. Employee engagement trends are significant because they link to many important performance outcomes crucial to organizational leaders such as productivity, employee retention, customer service, safety incidents, quality of work, and profitability.[12]

Based on the value employers (large and small) receive from One Medical, the company has grown its business customers from zero (in the days when Bruce Dunlevie and David Kennedy nudged Tom Lee to send a team member to promote One Medical to other businesses in One Medical's first downtown office) to over 9,400 businesses in 2024. The renewal rate for One Medical's business clients is 90%. Before the Amazon acquisition, more than 60% of all members came to One Medical through employers.

Amir Dan Rubin, One Medical's former CEO, describes the value employers receive this way:

> When I talked to employers about joining One Medical, I emphasized that we accepted their insurance and, for a nominal per-employee membership fee, could deliver cost-saving benefits through our team-based, human-centered, technology-powered primary care model. I also focused on how we would drive aware-ness and activation through our user-friendly app. For our most active clients, 81% of their employees download the app and sign up for services. From the perspective of active use, 45% of mem-bers interact with our technology (app or web version) each month. When we push a digital reminder for a task like a health screening, 50% of our members complete that task, and members average 11 engagements with One Medical annually.

So far, we've looked at One Medical's benefits to insurers and employ-ers using employer-sponsored healthcare plans. However, with the acquisi-tion of Iora Health in 2021, leaders at One Medical had to increase their focus on value creation for one of the United States' largest healthcare stakeholders—the Centers for Medicare & Medicaid Services (CMS). CMS is the government agency that oversees Medicare, Medicaid, the Children's Health Insurance Program (CHIP), and the Affordable Care Act (ACA) marketplaces. In the context of Iora, One Medical's service ecosystem expanded primarily to Medicare.

**QUICK CHECKUP**

Beyond cost savings, what types of value do you create for stakeholders? How is that value reflected in retention rates or relationship strength?

Iora Health was launched in 2010 by Chris McKown and Rushika Fernandopulle, MD, MPP, to restore humanity to healthcare by providing a "high-impact relationship-based care model that particularly benefits older adults on Medicare." Like One Medical, the model was designed to challenge the status quo by creating innovative solutions involving "the team, outcome-focused payment, customer service, and the technology that supports" senior care. In his acquisition announcement, Amir Dan Rubin noted Iora Health is "a technology-powered primary care leader delivering outstanding member-based, value-based care for adults 65+ enrolled in Medicare Advantage and other at-risk reimbursement models."

Medicare Advantage plans (Medicare Part C) are a comprehensive alternative to the original Medicare program. They are provided by private healthcare insurance companies and approved by Medicare. Typically, these plans bundle hospitalization, doctor/outpatient visits, and prescription coverage. In 2023, over half of Medicare recipients enrolled in a Medicare Advantage plan.

While most reimbursement models for younger patients are fee-based (the more services you provide, the more you bill), plans like Medicare Advantage are value-based (reimbursement is based on the provider's effectiveness in promoting health and preventing illness). Healthcare advisor Angie Howard, Vice President of Practice Solutions for Medical Advantage, describes value-based care this way:

Value-based care programs promote better healthcare for individuals, healthier lives for communities, and lower costs over time. Notably, they have been increasingly prominent since the ACA redirected focus toward measuring patient outcomes in contrast to quantifying the care administered without accountability. Value-based care is focused on providing care that is effective, applied judiciously, and documented accurately. Advocates of value-based care vs. fee-for-service say it improves patients' health and reduces healthcare costs.[13]

In short, value-based care links reimbursement to outcomes, and fee-based models link reimbursement to billable services (irrespective of outcomes). Despite CMS continually revising policies to encourage value-based care, a Deloitte Insights article suggests that "physician compensation continues to emphasize volume more than value . . . In 2020 . . . almost all physicians (97%) relied on FFS [fee for service] and/or salary for their compensation, and 36% also drew compensation from value-based payments."[14]

**One Medical Seniors**: Tech-Enabled Team-Based Care

One Medical has always paid its providers a salary. However, acquiring Iora Health made CMS a key stakeholder and required One Medical to demonstrate effectiveness as a value-based provider in the Medicare marketplace. By leveraging human-centered and technology-powered strengths,

One Medical developed comprehensive senior services integrating primary care providers, RN care managers, virtual medical teams, centralized and local support teams, and health coach navigators.

One Medical offers in-home care to seniors through practice care teams, home teams, social workers, health coaches, and nurses.

**Multi-Modal Care:** One Medical @ Home for Seniors

Home Team
NP - in home assessments;
Medical director - program
oversight, clinical support

Practice Care Team
Same-day needs
In-clinic needs
Behavioral health services

Social Worker
Psychosocial assessments
Resource needs
Family conflict resolution

Nurse
Care coordination
Disease management
Care planning
Triage

Health Coach
Care coordination
Outreach
Scheduling

Given One Medical's integrated team approach, the company demonstrates effectiveness in the Medicare value-based model. Writing for William Blair, a financial services company, industry analysts Ryan Daniels, CFA, and Jared Haase, CFA, declared One Medical (Iora Health) a big winner, "generating some of the highest gross savings' rates in the entire program [and] perhaps indicating an advantage to the pure-play center-based care operators compared to the provider enablement companies . . . More specifically, Iora Health generated gross savings of $42 million (a 23.9% gross savings rate) across a patient base of 12,038 lives . . ." Impressive numbers, but how did One Medical achieve them, and what is the human impact?

Anjali Jameson, One Medical's SVP of Product, has been actively involved with the Iora integration and notes:

It has been a meaningful challenge to combine a membership-based primary care model with a senior health value-based care business.

One Medical has always treated seniors—there's never been an age limit to membership. However, in the context of Iora, we treat a population of seniors. That means we must provide more and different care in a model that allows us to align the incentives to keep people well and maximally functional. We're providing team-based solutions that engage resources beyond the walls of One Medical. As we provide quality collaborative care in a value-based model, we apply what we have learned to One Medical's membership and fee-based services.

## ADDING THE QUALITATIVE TO THE QUANTITATIVE

I've shared financial and outcome data that shows how One Medical creates value for payors, employers, and the people those payors and employers serve. Before we shift to the value One Medical provides to other stakeholders, let's get a qualitative sense of what One Medical means to its business clients.

Phillip Sanders, Chief Operating Officer of MVP Law, a regional defense law firm with offices in seven Midwestern states, shares the value his firm receives from One Medical.

Our health plan covers about 350 people. Since we are self-insured, we have considerable leeway to create solutions customized to our employees and their families. As an employer of choice, families are a critical focus for our benefit solutions.

We have been with One Medical since 2018 and are fortunate to have two Kansas City clinics offering family medicine to everyone, from children to seniors. We understand the importance of having a primary care physician as a quarterback for acute and long-term healthcare needs.

From my perspective, the future of healthcare is reliant on patients establishing strong primary care relationships, and One Medical has been incredibly beneficial to MVP Law on that front.

MVP Law is focused on proactive and preventative care across physical, mental, and financial pillars. The savings we derive from working with One Medical are reinvested in other team member benefits. Our people are passionate about One Medical and share comments like, "Please ensure we can continue to receive care from the River Market clinic because that team knows us and our children love them."

Greg Golub is the CEO of Sequoia, an advisory firm that helps its business clients "get the most from their investment in people" by helping clients craft compensation, benefits, and overall people programs that meet their clients' business objectives. Greg explains the long-standing relationship between Sequoia and One Medical.

We've partnered with One Medical for more than 10 years to keep Sequoia's people healthy and productive and ensure One Medical's offerings are available to our clients. At Sequoia, our roughly 1,100 people have easy access to One Medical's high-quality, service-focused care. Also, roughly 1,200 of our clients use One Medical to support their people's health, productivity, and retention.

For example, we advised a large transportation company to use One Medical and followed that recommendation with a claims analysis. We looked at comparable segments of their workforce— some that had access to One Medical and some that did not. Longitudinal findings validated other results, showing that One Medical drove down costs over time.

Anecdotally, One Medical's primary care relationships have helped many clients' employees avert things like major cardiac issues by early detection of hypertension and avoided costly claims by helping other people get their blood sugar under control. A leader of one of our clients recently experienced leg issues while traveling. Thanks to One Medical, they had an immediate virtual appointment. The provider looked at their leg and advised them to receive immediate treatment for a blood clot that could have resulted in the loss of the leg or even death—if they hadn't taken care of the issue with urgency.

Similarly, Justworks (a professional employer organization—PEO—that helps entrepreneurs and smaller employers provide large group benefits to their employees) offers One Medical memberships to its team members and includes One Medical in health insurance packages for Justworks' clients. David Feinberg, Senior Vice President of Risk and Insurance at Justworks, explains:

> We have over 12,000 small business clients, each with an average of about 17 employees. In total, over 170,000 members are enrolled in our health plans, and we bundle access to One Medical for everyone who gets health insurance.
>
> One Medical was one of our first partner relationships, and the ease of care access coupled with their highly satisfying service have made them particularly attractive to our clients. The relationship with One Medical has been awesome for Justworks team members and the employers we serve. One Medical continues to receive high Net Promoter Score ratings in terms of the care received from individual providers and the overall experience with One Medical. Most engagements with One Medical are virtual. However, in locations where One Medical has physical offices, our clients benefit from having their people find and develop relationships with well-selected primary care providers that offer unrushed appointments and guide them to specialty care as needed.

On a personal basis, David notes:

> One Medical offers an incredible balance of humanity and technology. For example, I reached out for care while on vacation. With two sick kids in the back of the car and feeling sick myself, I used

the One Medical app to communicate with a clinician asynchronously. I didn't need to take an entire day out of the vacation to get throat cultures. That virtual visit interaction helped us get back to health quickly and more comfortably.

Greg and David both view One Medical's "human-powered and technology-aided" approach as aligned with how their respective businesses seek to operate. Greg shares:

Sequoia provides tech-enabled advisors who do much more because we've invested heavily in technology. That technology modernizes our industry and enables us to be where our clients are—when they need us. Comparably, One Medical has revolutionized the traditional doctor's office into a tech-enabled, preventive, and primary care network.

David puts it this way:

The PEO industry has been around for 40 years, helping businesses with payroll, HR compliance, and benefits. Since switching providers can be painful and expensive, the industry hasn't kept up with the technology or prioritized service. More than 10 years ago, Justworks built our own technology and committed to providing unparalleled service. We're the first in our sector to offer 24/7 support, and our customers and their employees can reach us through Slack, chat, or phone. That commitment to service, client satisfaction, access, and the revolutionary use of technology aligns with One Medical.

You know you create sustainable value for your service ecosystem when stakeholders view you as aligned with their values and desired outcomes.

Before we explore value creation for One Medical's healthcare partners and members, let's look at how you can apply lessons from One Medical to ensure you are Winning Through People & Technology.

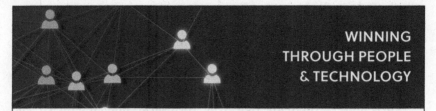

## HEALTHCARE SYSTEM GROWTH

Mother Teresa said, "I can do things you cannot; you can do things I cannot; together, we can do great things." She shared this thought while caring for patients living with HIV/AIDS, tuberculosis, and leprosy, but her words apply to all partnerships.

In the preceding section, we examined value creation for business clients and other payors. Let's examine how One Medical creates "win-win" value for health network partners.

The One Medical Board selected Amir Dan Rubin as CEO in 2017 because of his potential to grow the company through strategic partnerships. Benchmark Partner and then One Medical Board member Bruce Dunlevie explains:

In the early days, One Medical created healthcare partnerships in San Francisco that enabled us to streamline referrals to specialists and join our partners' insurance panels. However, we didn't have a systematic approach to building those partnerships across the country until Amir came on board. He deeply understood the needs of others in the healthcare delivery system, having worked as a Chief Operating Officer at UCLA Health Systems, Chief Executive Officer at Stanford Health, and an executive at UnitedHealth/Optum. He also had the insight, energy, and connections to take One Medical from a medium-sized business, professionalize the company, and turn it into a larger enterprise.

One Medical's shift to strategically forging partnerships is in keeping with broadly applicable guidance shared by Ruth De Backer and Eileen Kelly Rinaudo of McKinsey:

Partnerships never go out of style. Companies regularly seek partners with complementary capabilities to gain access to new markets and channels, share intellectual property or infrastructure, or reduce risk. The more complex the business environment becomes—for instance, as new technologies emerge or as innovation cycles get faster—the more such relationships make sense. And the better companies get at managing individual relationships, the more likely it is that they will become "partners of choice" and able to build entire portfolios of practical and value-creating partnerships.[15]

**QUICK CHECKUP**

With whom might you partner to:

- gain access to new markets or channels,
- share intellectual property or infrastructure, and
- reduce risk?

For One Medical to "get better" at forging partnerships, Amir recruited healthcare colleagues to the company. A crucial part of that recruitment was John Singerling. John, One Medical's Chief Network Officer, had a 23-year career in healthcare before joining One Medical—the last nine years of which he served as the president of the largest healthcare system in South Carolina. John explained his decision to join One Medical, noting:

> I'd known and respected Amir for years, and our leadership team read the book you wrote about working with Amir at UCLA— *Prescription for Excellence.* A merger of my healthcare system would have required my family to relocate, but Amir offered me an opportunity to disrupt and reinvent healthcare without disrupting my family. While One Medical's early innovation in designing a human-centered in-person and virtual primary care model was a strategic differentiator, Amir brought me in to scale and link our model to leading health systems in strategic regions. Given invest-ments from the Carlyle Group and others, we had the capital to expand our footprint and scale our impact.

Using best principles in partnership strategy, One Medical leaders:

1. Prioritized new regions,
2. Identified ideal health system partners in those regions,
3. Engaged and listened to the needs of prospective partners,
4. Shared One Medical's vision and desired outcomes from the partnership,
5. Negotiated the deal terms and partnership legal agreements,
6. Designed a partnership launch and implementation playbook, and
7. Built infrastructure needed to execute and measure the success of the collaboration.

From the perspective of new market prioritization, One Medical tar-geted large urban areas. John notes:

> We primarily targeted expansion into some of America's largest cities, although we also sought to prove our model could work in

mid-sized geographies. We analyzed the demographic profiles of individuals and business clients most interested in a membership-based primary care offering and used algorithms to rank the geographies for those profiles. We wanted to be in areas where we had the greatest opportunity to garner brand recognition and provide people with One Medical's refreshing and differentiated approach compared to the typical fragmented and frustrating healthcare experience.

Upon completing their market analysis, Amir, John, and a core group of One Medical team members identified and approached prospective health system partners in those geographies. The One Medical team met with leaders at compatible health systems to assess their interest in forming a health network or health system partnership. People like John listened to the needs of the local health system leaders and shared One Medical's goals and points of differentiation. These healthcare leaders typically needed more primary care access and providers who could coordinate care with the system's specialists and hospitals. Conversely, to improve the member and provider experience, One Medical needed to seamlessly connect its care model to the diagnostic and specialty services not offered in One Medical brick-and-mortar clinics. One Medical also benefited from being under the payor umbrella of the local healthcare network—meaning that One Medical wouldn't need to negotiate reimbursement terms with insurance companies.

The process of courting and signing agreements with network partners is time-consuming. One Medical leaders went from initial exploration to a signed contract with some network providers in 12 to 18 months, while other partnership agreements took five years to secure. Generally, within 18 months of signing an agreement, One Medical opened two to three clinics in that market to provide geographic coverage. John Singerling adds, "National and regional employers let us know where they want us to open clinics to provide benefit parity to their employees whenever possible. Their input is part of our algorithm to identify new geographies and clinic locations within those areas." At the time of this writing, One Medical has more than 240 primary care offices in more than 21 US locations (*see figure below*), covering roughly 50% of the US population.

Chapter 4 will explore how One Medical creates additional value for its network partners by streamlining the secure transfer of patient information. Chapter 7 will examine Amazon's plans for One Medical's market growth. For now, let's hear directly from a couple of One Medical network partners.

Shelby Decosta, MHA, is the President of the University of California, San Francisco's (UCSF) healthcare network. UCSF Health, One Medical's first health partner, is an academic medical network comprised of the Helen Diller Medical Center at Parnassus Heights, UCSF Medical Center at Mount Zion, UCSF Medical Center at Mission Bay, UCSF Benioff Children's Hospitals in Oakland and San Francisco, and Helen Diller Family Comprehensive Cancer Center. It also includes the UCSF Weill Institute for Neurosciences, which consists of the Langley Porter Psychiatric Hospital and Clinics, UCSF Benioff Children's Physicians, and the UCSF Faculty Practice.

Shelby, who manages affiliate relationships, oversees network operations and clinical quality, and ensures successful alignment with UCSF Health's priorities, explains the synergies that attracted UCSF to One Medical:

In 2010, when the relationship started, while we were very focused on caring for the sickest, most complex patients, those patients also had primary care needs. As we looked for a patient-oriented primary care partner, One Medical was there. One Medical focused on things like making care easy in ways that traditional health systems and academic medical centers typically did not. Back in 2010, that included creating multiple ways for patients to communicate with providers and offering same-day or next-day appointments. They had excellent support staff and care teams that maximized the time providers spent with their patients.

Fast-forwarding to the present, Shelby suggests the original value drivers remain in place, plus:

The benefits of our partnership are based on earned trust. We work to ensure seamless experiences and the integration of patient records. For example, teams at UCSF and One Medical look at ways to streamline high volumes of referrals in areas like cardiology. One Medical providers triage those referrals—so our cardiology teams understand the urgency with which the referral needs to be seen. Our cardiologists also know that a patient referred from One Medical is vetted with complete information provided.

Similarly, Lynn Stofer, President of Mass General Brigham Community Physicians, expresses the value her organization receives from its partnership with One Medical. Mass General Brigham, affiliated with Harvard University, is the largest hospital-based research system in the world. It provides a "continuum of care across a system of academic medical centers, community and specialty hospitals, a health insurance plan, physician networks, community health centers, home care, and long-term care services. Mass General Brigham is a nonprofit organization committed to patient care, research, teaching, and service to the community."[16]

Lynn shares her views on the value One Medical brings to Mass General Brigham:

Around 2019, One Medical approached us. We'd been tracking them and saw them as an emerging company that disruptively tackled challenges in primary care. Given the size of our organization and the need to ensure that One Medical wasn't competing with our physicians but rather offering a complementary option for patients seeking primary care, it took 18 to 20 months to vet them and sign our agreement. We knew they had a solid primary care base, were innovative, and their Net Promoter Scores were off the chart. So, our goal was to partner with them to grow together. They could help us enhance primary care access, and we wanted to learn from their innovative and patient-centric practices while benefiting from their ability to stand up practices. They also had great relationships with employers who looked to One Medical to provide their employees with technology tools, an inviting practice environment, and a human-centric care model.

Through the years, Lynn has been impressed by One Medical's knowledge, transparency, and reliability:

They've made promises to us and kept them. They follow through and get things done. Their 24/7 access has been great. They greet and treat patients competently and compassionately. One Medical leaders have partnered with us for reliable governance, and I love working with and learning from them. We hope that Amazon's acquisition will help us partner on a local, regional, and even national scale.

One Medical leaders continue to improve their ability to forge partnerships and increase the speed of new clinic openings in those locations. They have also established an evidence-based track record (and testimonials like the ones provided by Lynn and Shelby), demonstrating the benefits prospective healthcare systems can receive. Like all relationships, leaders at One Medical continually assess and address the changing needs of their partners to ensure sustainable success.

## CLINICAL OUTCOME VALUE AND POPULATION HEALTH

One Medical's "human-centric" and "transformative" value proposition emerged from Dr. Tom Lee's desire to make the primary care patient experience easier, more accessible, and increasingly effective. In chapters 4 and 5, you will read examples of how individual patients experience ease, accessibility, and positive clinical outcomes through One Medical's design and deployment of people, processes, and technology, but before we end this chapter, let's look at how One Medical creates value through innovation and clinical research focused on population health.

The term "population health" was advanced by Robert Evans and Greg Stoddart in 1990 and defined operationally in a 2003 *American Journal of Public Health* article coauthored by Stoddart and David Kindig. In that article (titled "What Is Population Health?"), Kindig and Stoddart suggest:

> Population health is a relatively new term that has not yet been precisely defined. Is it a concept of health or a field of study of health determinants? We propose that the definition be "the health outcomes of a group of individuals, including the distribution of such outcomes within the group," and we argue that the field of population health includes health outcomes, patterns of health determinants, and policies and interventions that link these two . . . These populations are often geographic regions, such as nations or communities, but they can also be other groups, such as employees . . . many determinants of health, such as medical care systems, the social environment, and the physical environment, have their biological impact on individuals in part at a population level.

Given that One Medical's membership model covers roughly a million members of diverse ages and cultural backgrounds from across the United States connected through an integrated health record and mobile application, the company is well positioned to study health determinants and the impact of innovations in healthcare delivery.

Raj Behal, MD, left roles as Chief Quality Officer and Associate Dean of Quality/Adult Clinical Services at the Stanford University School of Medicine to help One Medical improve population health for its members and publish research so patients outside One Medical could benefit. Raj explains:

> When I came to One Medical in 2017, my team and I looked at how One Medical could broadly maximize our impact on the lives of members and healthcare patients. In addition to establishing guidelines and protocols for our members' myriad primary care issues, we took a systematic and structured approach to addressing common conditions that lead to the greatest morbidity and mortality. We started by focusing on heart disease and cancer, along with other mental health and musculoskeletal conditions that significantly affect patients' quality of life.

Raj, One Medical's Chief Quality Officer, and his team quickly identified opportunities to improve outcomes for One Medical's diabetic population. Specifically, One Medical sought to improve performance against Healthcare Effectiveness Data and Information Set (HEDIS) guidelines regarding the number of patients poorly controlling their HbA1c (greater than 9.0%). Since proper blood sugar monitoring can avert major health conditions like heart disease, kidney disease, and vision loss, Raj's team (working with One Medical clinicians specializing in diabetes care) developed an integrated treatment program to increase HbA1c control. That program, part of a larger chronic condition management program One Medical calls IMPACT, deploys a range of clinical professionals, methods, and tools to help One Medical members maximize control over their blood sugar.

One Medical clinicians refer patients to the program consisting of specialty clinicians, health coaches, and virtual medical professionals. Participants receive months of education and support. One Medical, an early adopter of remote devices, deploys continuous glucose monitors (CGMs) to help program participants translate the food they eat into recorded fluctuations in blood sugars. The support team provides group classes and regular contact with the participants and tailors evidence-based recommendations to each participant's lifestyle and values. The IMPACT team does not prescribe "diets." Instead, they help patients learn to self-regulate blood sugars through real-time monitoring and applying blood-sugar-regulating principles like eating whole foods. Throughout the program, the One Medical primary care physician remains actively informed about their patient's progress via the shared health record.

While reflecting on the IMPACT program, Raj notes:

Our outcomes are among the best in the country for improving blood sugar control. We're at the 95th percentile, and the benchmark doesn't go higher. Also, these improvements show no disparity by gender, race, or ethnicity. Which, based on my research knowledge, is extremely rare. We have shown that our results also positively impact healthcare costs [see figure on next page] and have published our findings so other healthcare systems can empower similar improvements. We've also broadened our IMPACT model to address Cardiometabolic Health, focusing on early intervention for pre-diabetes and heart disease risk.

Hemalee Patel, MD, a member of Raj's clinical effectiveness team, highlights an added benefit One Medical providers receive from referring their patients to the IMPACT program:

As a provider, I appreciate it when I don't have to increase a patient's insulin, and I am especially pleased when I can decrease or eliminate it. Also, when chronic conditions like diabetes come under control, I can spend less time talking about that condition and invest more energy in building a proactive and holistic patient relationship.

**Employers:** Outsized diabetes results for better health

One Medical is proven to deliver better HbA1c outcomes for our patients ...

... which, in turn, impact the bottom line for employers.[7]

| Solution | Nominal Reduction (% points) |
|---|---|
| One Medical[1] | 2.0 pt |
| Virta[2] | 1.3 pt |
| Livongo[3] | 1.1 pt |
| Lark[4] | 1.1 pt |
| Omada[5] | 0.8 pt |
| Abbott[6] | 0.6 pt |

| 1% ⬇ | 1.7% ⬇ | 7% ⬇ |
|---|---|---|
| HbA1c | All-cause total health care costs | Diabetes-related total healthcare costs |

One Medical's clinical effectiveness team has innovated and measured the success of other cost- and time-saving solutions, such as a virtual physical therapy program called "Motion." Benchmarking against national data, the Motion program resolves conditions requiring physical therapy in half the visits (five as opposed to 10), with 98% of members saying they would refer the program to family and friends.

With the encouragement of a large employer, One Medical launched a Healthy Mind program to address mental health issues that don't rise to the level of a clinical diagnosis of depression or generalized anxiety disorder. These issues might include mental fog, increased stress, or sleep disturbance. Working with Creyos Health, One Medical offers a digital cognitive test with tailored behavioral recommendations and structured support. Upon completing the Healthy Mind program, participants show substantial improvements on post-program cognitive tests. In addition to these evidence-based benefits, members report increased confidence and comfort with managing their health.

One Medical continues to explore ways to leverage "human-centered and technology-powered" innovation to create value for individual patients, member populations, and US healthcare overall. For example, members turning 40 receive a push alert through their app encouraging them to schedule a Healthy Heart visit. Since lifestyle modification often prevents heart disease, One Medical's Healthy Heart assessment is leading edge and more aggressive than the existing US Preventive Services Task Force (USPSTF) guidelines. One Medical's triggered push alerts (like the Healthy Heart assessment, breast cancer screens, and mammograms) routinely receive a 22%–30% completion rate within two weeks. A reminder alert typically results in an additional 20% of members completing the task.

Raj Behal notes, "I was honestly surprised by the results of our technology-powered outreach. Ultimately, I think our success comes from the relationships our providers build with patients and the power of electronically nudging people to manage their health proactively."

Before we close the chapter with a patient story that demonstrates One Medical's value creation across the service ecosystem, let's look at how you can apply lessons from One Medical to ensure you are Winning Through People & Technology.

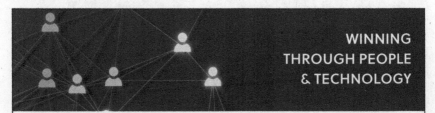

## WINNING THROUGH PEOPLE & TECHNOLOGY

1. Who are your company's or department's most important strategic partners?
2. How are you evaluating and increasing partnership success?
3. When you consider new partnerships, what is your process for:
   a. Prioritizing geographies,
   b. Identifying ideal partners,
   c. Listening to the needs of prospects,
   d. Sharing your desired outcomes, and
   e. Building the infrastructure needed to execute and measure success?

---

4. To what degree do you evaluate the value you provide for specific groups of individuals you serve (e.g., your version of population health)? What are those groups, and what value do you provide them?

5. To what degree do you share your successes so that others can benefit from your process improvements and innovations?

---

## WHEN IT ALL COMES TOGETHER

To appreciate how creating value across the service ecosystem produces transformational results, let's look at a story shared by Alani Gregory, MD. Dr. Gregory's existing patient used the One Medical app to book an appointment for cold symptoms. In addition to having symptoms of an upper respiratory infection, the patient complained of mild neck pain. Alani checked the patient's lymph nodes and noted swelling (lymphadenopathy) consistent with the infection. She offered a course of treatment, but 10 days later, the patient made an urgent, same-day appointment because her symptoms had worsened.

Given Alani's knowledge of the patient, she noticed a change in her voice and observed significant growth in the patient's thyroid. Because of One Medical's partnership with a local healthcare system, Alani contacted the healthcare partner's radiology team and scheduled the patient for a CT scan the next day. As soon as the scan was completed, the radiologist immediately let Alani know that the patient appeared to have an aggressive cancer that required prompt attention. Alani promptly contacted network partners to identify the best possible provider for her patient. Upon discussing the case with the selected endocrinologist, Alani contacted the patient. She advised her of the findings, offered support, and guided her on the steps.

Alani notes:

I told the patient to go to the hospital emergency room, where the specialist would receive her and ensure she got the care she needed. She said, "I didn't believe you because I've heard so many bad stories about the emergency room. But I walked in, and everyone was immediately on top of me, including the head of the emergency room. They knew who I was."

Within two weeks of the cancer diagnosis, Alani's patient had started chemotherapy. From Alani's perspective, experiences like this reinforce her passion for providing primary care.

To put the two-week initiation of chemo timeline into perspective, a peer-reviewed study published in *PLOS One* utilized data from the National Cancer Database for newly diagnosed US cancer patients to determine TTI or Time to Initiation of first treatment after diagnosis. While TTI varies by cancer type, all wait times were substantially longer than what Alani's patient experienced. The researchers also observed, "TTI has lengthened significantly and is associated with absolute increased risk of mortality ranging from 1.2–3.2% per week in curative settings such as early-stage breast, lung, renal, and pancreas cancers. Studies of interventions to ease navigation and reduce barriers are warranted to diminish potential harm to patients."[17]

In this example, Dr. Gregory's patient had a swift connection to diagnostics, specialists, and treatment and is now in remission. The partner healthcare system provided life-saving care, and the streamlined process saved insurance providers money—since Dr. Gregory's patient didn't seek treatment for her worsening condition in an emergency room. That's how human-centered and technology-powered care produces results across the service ecosystem! What can it do in yours?

Before we look at how to design and execute a human-centric and technology-powered strategy, let's take a moment to look at this chapter's Transformational Lessons.

## TRANSFORMATIONAL LESSONS

- Don Tapscott suggests, "In an age where everything and everyone is linked through networks of glass and air, no one—no business, organization, government agency, country—is an island. We need to do right by all our stakeholders."
- Organizations should consider their "value networks"—beneficial connections with other organizations and individuals.
- A vital business tension involves reducing costs without compromising quality.
- Mother Teresa observed, "I can do things you cannot; you can do things I cannot; together, we can do great things."
- A successful partnership strategy has five components: (1) prioritizing new locations, (2) identifying ideal partners, (3) listening to the needs of prospects, (4) sharing desired outcomes, (5) negotiating the partnership, (6) designing the launch and implementation playbook, and (7) building infrastructure to execute and measure collaborative success.
- Producing verifiable results for existing partners facilitates future partner acquisition.
- In addition to the benefits companies provide to individual customers, they should consider a "population health" approach where they aggregate benefits for core customer segments.
- Highly innovative companies are comfortable sharing their breakthroughs and learning from the breakthroughs of others.
- Human-centered and technology-powered care can produce results for all service ecosystem stakeholders.

# Innovative Design and Execution

# Designing Human-Centered and Technology-Powered Solutions

*The best design is the simplest one that works.*

**Albert Einstein, theoretical physicist[1]**

## HUMAN DESIGN

As a human experience designer who helps leaders and frontline team members craft experiences that emotionally engage and drive loyalty for their value networks (colleagues, customers, clients, and partners), I am inspired by the process and insights of Tim Brown, former CEO and co-chair of IDEO.

For over 40 years, IDEO, a global design firm, has helped brands apply design thinking to innovate solutions that maintain each brand's relevance and sustainability. Tim views design and innovation this way: "Where you innovate, how you innovate, and what you innovate are design problems."[2]

In this chapter, I provide an overview of design thinking; explore how that thinking guides design at One Medical; spotlight One Medical's people, process, and technology innovations; and offer ideas on how you can apply insights garnered from One Medical to your human-centered and technology-powered solutions. The former president of IBM, Thomas J. Watson Jr., once said, "Good design is good business."[3] In that spirit, let's review the steps needed to produce "good design"—whether you are crafting products, technologies, or human interactions.

## GOOD DESIGN DOESN'T HAPPEN BY DEFAULT

The Interaction Design Foundation defines design thinking as a "nonlinear, iterative process" used in a team context to understand the needs of others, question assumptions, redefine problems, and craft trial solutions refined through testing. To derive the benefits of design thinking, designers (anyone seeking to solve a business problem) should follow a circular, five-phase process:

1. **Empathize**—Research the needs of those whose problems you are trying to solve. Challenge your assumptions and biases. Suspend judgment to understand your target audience's stated and unstated wants, needs, desires, and preferences.

2. **Define**—Analyze the information gathered in the "empathize" phase and synthesize those inputs into concise **problem statements** (also called **points of view—POV**). To further humanize the problem statements, frame them in the context of **personas** (fictional characters created from customer segmentation research). A persona typically reflects a group's demographics (general characteristics like gender, age, and income), psychographics (interests, attitudes, values, opinions, and lifestyles), experiences, needs, goals, and behaviors.

3. **Ideate**—Brainstorm (generate without filters or judgment) ways to resolve each problem statement. Push for ideas that reflect both

incremental and novel approaches to problem resolution. Foster an environment where people boldly share possibilities that might address the root cause of problems.

4. **Prototype**—From the brainstormed idea list, look for solutions with the greatest potential to effectively and impactfully address each problem statement. Create rudimentary, low-cost ways to investigate your solutions.

5. **Test**—Evaluate each prototype with individuals representing the persona for which the solution was crafted. As feedback is garnered from testing, reengage the steps by *empathizing* with that feedback, *redefining* problem statements, *ideating* iterative improvements to the designs, revising *prototypes* based on that creativity, and *testing* the revised prototypes.

While the design process is straightforward, front-end developer Brian Reed reminds us, "Everything is designed. Few things are designed well."[4] So, let's look at how One Medical uses design thinking and consistent processes to design well.

## THE ONE MEDICAL WAY

Given that One Medical's unique value proposition (UVP) involves maximizing access to primary care, making it easy for people to get their needs met, and creating personalized connections between stakeholders, One Medical designers focus on experience design by collaboratively developing products, services, and environments.

Amy Livingston, Director of Model Experience, provides a high-level overview of One Medical's experience design structure, noting, "Our product teams essentially focus on the member experience through the app, the care team's experience through the electronic health record, and member experiences either during physical office or virtual visits."

Austin Hastings, Senior Director of Product Design at One Medical, adds:

We often think of the product development team as involving a core triad of product management, engineers, and design and research, who work closely throughout the end-to-end product process for strategic and tactical success. Magic happens when these roles bring their strengths and unique perspectives to understand the desirability, viability, and feasibility of concepts at the right points in the process. This helps us more quickly ensure we're not only solving something the right way but we're also solving the right thing in the first place. It's also crucial to work collaboratively across the organization to deepen perspectives on the problem spaces in which we work, engaging with partners along the way, such as clinical, marketing, operations, support teams, leadership, and more. We've sought to correct for problems that come from design organizations being too centralized or disconnected from the planning and prioritization process by working to integrate research and human-centered design earlier in planning processes.

Kyle Munkittrick, Group Product Manager at One Medical, explains the distinction between software and experiential design:

We look at design holistically and include the physicality and service elements of the experience wherever possible. As software designers, we can sometimes focus on bits and bytes in front of us. However, at One Medical, we observe care as it is provided. For example, as a patient checks in, we are considering whether we need to change how the office is shaped. What do our medical support specialists say to the patients as they walk in? As we are prototyping AI software that records the interaction of a patient and a clinician in the exam room, we are considering how the clinician can best explain and get the patient's permission for that recording as they walk them down the hall to the exam room.

Given One Medical's brand differentiators, experience designers seek to leverage technology, products, processes, and people to create **access,**

**convenience**, and **personalization**. These design targets align well with what analysts describe as Amazon's core experience differentiators. Writing for FourWeekMBA.com, Guerric de Ternay notes that Amazon's unique value "encompasses a wide range of services, features, and customer-centric elements designed to provide convenience, selection, and cost-effectiveness in online shopping and related sectors. Amazon's value proposition is characterized by its customer obsession, extensive product catalog, fast and reliable delivery, digital services, and customer-centric innovation."[5] We will examine the core values driving Amazon's differentiation in chapter 7. For now, let's focus on a design outcome that One Medical and Amazon desire—**accessibility**.

From the perspective of access, long-standing One Medical CEO Amir Dan Rubin focused on five "*As*" of access based on a framework created by Roy Penchansky and J. William Thomas (two professors Amir encountered while receiving his MBA from the University of Michigan). That framework suggests access is the degree of fit between a consumer and a service in five key areas:

1. **Accessibility**—Is the service within reasonable proximity of the consumer?
2. **Availability**—Is there sufficient supply to meet consumer demand?
3. **Acceptability**—Does the service align with the attitudes and cultural needs of the customer?
4. **Affordability**—Is the provider able to deliver the service affordably and profitably?
5. **Adequacy or Accommodation**—Is the service designed for usability (organized and accommodating to users)?[6]

Amir notes that One Medical designs member experiences to address these access dimensions:

From the perspective of accessibility and availability—we've created workflows that enable same- and next-day appointments and virtual care in minutes. We strive to create an environment where clinicians want to practice so we can meet the needs of our members. Our focus on accessibility means we make primary care a click away or available near where members work, shop, and live. We address accommodation by considering the members' perspectives and asking questions from their point of view. These are questions like, "Does this app, service, or human interaction meet my needs?" "Does it address my preferences, and is it tailored to serve people like me?" We've addressed affordability through our nominal fee-based membership model, which enables us to provide on-demand, virtual care for no deductible or an added fee. Since accommodation often equates to office hours or providing services consistent with the lifestyle of those you serve, our 24/7 asynchronous and synchronous availability reflects an accommodating fit.

When I first consulted for One Medical in 2018, design teams were looking at access, convenience, and personalization opportunities across the longitudinal journeys of stakeholders. This process initially involved identifying, evaluating, and elevating interaction moments (touchpoints) for One Medical patient/member segments. The phases evaluated included:

- Joining
- Onboarding and establishing care
- Sustaining health and strengthening relationship
- Renewing relationship

Will Kimbrough, MD, Vice President of Strategic Clinical Services at One Medical, suggests that many of the company's design efforts are dedicated to helping members navigate their care.

Healthcare is messy, and we try to clean up that mess as much as possible. As a primary care physician, I don't always know where to send a patient, but somebody in my ecosystem does. I work in this system every day, and if I can't easily navigate it, patients don't stand a chance on their own. So, we design experiences that guide people through their journeys. Ideally, we do it all in the same tech stack and ecosystem. However, given the nature of this industry, people will need specialists, and Labcorp or Quest will run some labs. So, we'll continue to look at ways to streamline integrated experiences and make a patient's next step as obvious as possible.

Similarly, Austin Hastings, Senior Director of Product Design, describes his journey with the company and how One Medical strives to clean up the "messiness of healthcare" through touchpoint and longitudinal journey design.

I've been on the design team at One Medical for three and a half years; before that, I was a member of One Medical for seven years. As a member, I was impressed by my seamless and easy experience and how this felt like how healthcare should be. As an employee, I've been impressed with our human-centered approach to the many touchpoints across a member's healthcare journey. That human-centricity is embedded in the company's DNA. In the broader world of healthcare, patient journeys are often fragmented and, at times, can even be frightening and painful. At One Medical, we use a mental model of longitudinal care, where the provider and patient journey goes through different paths at different times, from annual exams to chronic care needs to episodic care that is still connected with a patient's overall care. As designers, we have the tool kit to help teams better understand and simplify healthcare's complexity, designing to identify and solve for key patient delta moments, and to visualize and deeply understand how to design and deliver optimal One Medical journeys.

By Austin's definition, delta moments occur when primary care doesn't meet the needs of patients or when One Medical members experience frustration or friction. Austin adds:

We spend a lot of time seeking to understand what people expect, need, and feel and where an experience falls short. We meet with patients and providers to watch the care being delivered. We document what we observe and brainstorm possible solutions in cross-functional teams of designers, engineers, product managers, analysts, customer support specialists, clinical providers, practice managers, and more. We look for iterative solutions but also seek to raise the bar in imagining the ideal healthcare experience. Through vision and exploratory projects, we are imagining and mapping aspirational journeys. We collaboratively storyboard those aspirations and engage illustrators to bring the storyboards to life, which can then inspire and influence further design discovery and research and, more broadly, help team members understand the potential of our offering. Through that aspirational process, we are answering the question, what should longitudinal care look like for patients and care teams? How can we differentiate it, how can we make it better and easier, and how can we deliver improved health outcomes? We take both the patient and care team perspectives and experiences into account to ensure we create a great patient and provider experience.

Unlike many other brands that create journey maps only for customers (and may consider service providers incidentally), One Medical leaders and designers assess the journey of varied stakeholders. For example, the One Medical employee (people) experience is examined across:

- Selection
- Onboarding
- Development/retention
- Transition

The Harvard Business School Online summarizes the benefits of employee journey mapping as:

- Visualizing each employee's experience at your company

- Illuminating holes or areas for improvement in your current employee experience
- Enabling more accurate job descriptions
- Informing budget allocation for initiatives that boost retention and engagement

Each of these helps increase employee satisfaction—thus increasing their motivation and quality of work—and your company's competitive edge in the talent search.[7]

**QUICK CHECKUP**

Are you using tools like journey maps? Have you crafted maps for multiple customer segments and other stakeholders—such as employees?

At One Medical, the journey mapping process spotlights opportunities for "good design" at high-value interaction moments (often referred to as "moments of truth"). Behavioral economic research from Nobel Prize–winning economist Daniel Kahneman, his colleague Amos Tversky, and others suggest that moments of truth are typically memorable and infused with emotion. Research-based, high-value moments include:

- **Arrivals**—Your customers' initial impressions of apps, websites, phone calls, and in-person visits establish whether they have arrived in the right place and feel welcome.
- **Transitions**—Customers are often anxious when they move from one phase to the next. For example, transitioning from sales to service can leave customers wondering, "Will they care for me as much after I've made a purchase?"
- **Pain**—High-effort moments and painful experiences are particularly memorable to customers—unless the pain is resolved well before an interaction ends.

- **Peak**—Positive emotions are significant and memorable—as long as painful moments don't overshadow or end an interaction.
- **Endings**—Customers tend to remember experiences that close an interaction.

Sally Ward, MD, offers an example of how One Medical designed a positive and personalized interaction at the *end* of the candidate experience. Sally notes, "We are committed to designing and delivering the best candidate experience in the world. So, in the clinical realm, we contact every candidate who applies and offer feedback to those who advance through the process but aren't selected." Many companies for whom I've consulted only respond to candidates that interest them, leaving the rest to wonder if their application was received, let alone reviewed.

**QUICK CHECKUP**

What are the "moments of truth" for your core customer segments, team members, and partners? How are you ensuring experience excellence in those moments?

For many organizations, design teams function as a shared resource. Individual departments request design services on a project basis and pay for them from their cost center. At One Medical, experience designers are members of service delivery teams. Designers target projects that surface from teams and leadership priorities. Austin explains:

> We respond to leadership's strategic priorities and the issues raised by clinical and support team members. We often focus on critical user journeys, like an annual physical, because they are ubiquitous and essential to patients' health.

Before we examine how One Medical's design approach has resulted in human-centric achievements, let's look at how you can apply lessons from One Medical to ensure you are Winning Through People & Technology.

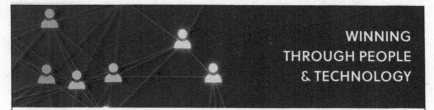

1. Assume good design is good for your business. How would you rate how your team, department, or organization crafts solutions? How does your "non-linear, iterative design process" contribute to your success?
2. What are your strengths and opportunities across each phase (empathize, define, ideate, prototype, test) of the design process? Think of concrete examples of your design strengths and opportunities.
3. Does your team, department, or organization use personas to guide design? If so, how effectively are they used? If not, what would it take to build personas that reflect core business segments?
4. One Medical's overarching design objectives are access, convenience, and personalization. What are yours?
5. Using the Penchansky and Thomas framework, how well do your products/services meet your customers' needs regarding accessibility, availability, acceptance, affordability, and adequacy or accommodation? In what areas are you working to maximize fit?

## ONE MEDICAL'S DESIGN SUCCESS

Stuart Parmenter, who served as One Medical's Chief Technology Officer (CTO), was the co-founder and CTO of Rise, a nutritional coaching platform that One Medical acquired in 2016. Previously, Stuart had worked for eight years for Mozilla (best known for its Firefox web browser). Given Stuart's long career in technology and senior leadership role with One Medical, he offers keen insights into One Medical's design breakthroughs. For context, when Stuart joined One Medical in 2016, a team of roughly 25 designers and technologists was rolling out face-to-face, video-based, on-demand care. This breakthrough technology evolved from earlier One Medical innovations that allowed members to securely communicate with providers through the One Medical app. Video-based care was being delivered as a convenience to One Medical members years before others adopted it during COVID-19. According to Stuart:

> We are committed to making it easier for providers to deliver and for members to receive care. We are always looking for ways to make that care accessible in the context of high-demand lifestyles. Our early deployment of video-based on-demand visits is less about technology and more about the outcomes we are trying to deliver through the tools we develop. Those outcomes should reduce complexity, increase ease, and foster access.

While the healthcare system is complicated (and prone to breakdowns), Stuart suggests that great design focuses on small changes that will likely have a high impact. For example, One Medical has invested considerable time and money in automating its appointment system to streamline scheduling for members and One Medical staff. Stuart refers to these "small, high-value targets" *not* as low-hanging fruit but as fruit that has already fallen and needs to be collected for large-scale impact. While the targets appear small, the backstage design and development work needed to drive impact is sizable. When it comes to scheduling, Stuart explains:

> We manage many moving parts so patients can easily access care. These include behind-the-scenes coordination of scheduling calendars and the member's desired care platform. We access every primary care provider's and virtual team member's availability. We then coordinate that with our member's desired treatment option (in person, scheduled virtual, or on-demand).

The importance of "small, high-value targets" like streamlining scheduling is evidenced in the Kyruus 2023 Care Access Benchmark Report, showing that 61% of patients view online scheduling as "extremely or very important." Of patients who didn't schedule their last appointment online,

34% said it was because the provider didn't have the technology or appointment times available. The authors of the Kyruus report added, "Expand your current online scheduling capabilities to route patients to advanced practice providers (PAs, NPs) for lower acuity care (e.g., flu shots) rather than a primary care physician. This not only improves capacity for the system but also opens up availability for patients seeking care."[8] That guidance has been One Medical's approach since the company started.

---

### QUICK CHECKUP

What are your "small, high-value" customer experience targets?

---

The broad lesson from Stuart's scheduling example is the importance of making it easy for prospects and customers to find, schedule, and do business with you. This enduring business principle is supported by data from 75,000 consumers published in the *Harvard Business Review* (*HBR*) by Matthew Dixon, Karen Freeman, and Nick Toman in 2010. In their article, "Stop Trying to Delight Your Customers," Dixon, Freeman, and Toman encouraged business leaders to focus on customer ease. The authors warned against having team members try to "exceed customer expectations" because that approach often results in higher costs and wasted effort. Instead, they recommend designing for customer ease. To do this, they suggest removing obstacles that get in the way of customer success. Specifically, they note:

> Customers resent having to contact the company repeatedly (or be transferred) to get an issue resolved, having to repeat information, and having to switch from one service channel to another . . . Companies can reduce these types of effort and measure the effects with a new metric, the Customer Effort Score (CES), which assigns ratings from 1 to 5, with 5 representing very high effort.[9]

The Customer Effort Score (CES) is generated by a single question that asks customers to rate how much effort they had to exert to get their needs met. CES correlates substantially higher with future customer purchases and increased spending than questions about customer satisfaction. CES also outperforms the popular customer experience metric, Net Promoter Score (NPS), in terms of future purchases and customer spending. (More on NPS in chapter 5.)

In the *HBR* article, Dixon, Freeman, and Toman specifically cite the frustration customers experience when they are transferred. One Medical addressed that challenge by investing in design solutions that ensure inbound communications from members are routed efficiently and effectively. Stuart provides further context by noting that early in One Medical's history, if a member sent a message to their provider about an insurance question, the provider would reroute it. That meant the message could be passed on multiple times before it got to the person best suited to answer it, and this could result in the member waiting a week for a response.

> Since then, we've built machine-learning models that analyze and route all inbound messages. Through that automation, we've removed work from the provider and all the individuals who had to look at the message before routing it elsewhere. While this might seem like a trivial design problem, the workflow savings across our entire network are huge. The time saved reading and forwarding these messages is time now available to provide care.

Stuart, who was a One Medical member before he joined and led the One Medical technology team, clearly frames the goal of One Medical's design approach and technology deployment—to improve the efficiency, scale, and quality of clinical *care*.

> Our job as a technology team in a care organization is to make healthcare more manageable and less complicated. So, from a leadership perspective, I needed to select and grow a human-centric design and development team. Since 2016, we have grown from 25 people in technology to 420. As we grew, we focused on the never-ending need to simplify the healthcare experience.

It's one thing to streamline appointments and improve communications within a business and quite another to collaborate with partners outside of your business to do the same. Let's examine One Medical's approach to ensuring "less effort" when accessing specialists and efficiently exchanging information with healthcare partners.

## INTEGRATING AND INTEGRATED EXPERIENCES

Most of us had parents and early educators who emphasized the importance of "sharing." While sharing is a highly valued quality, organizational silos, misaligned processes, and incompatible technologies create barriers. Customer experience (CX) writer Mike Henry distinguishes these challenges as either requiring an "integrated customer experience" or "CX integrations." By integrated customer experience, Mike is referring to breaking down data silos and bringing together diverse customer data into a centralized location. Customer experience integration aims to create a comprehensive view of the customer so insights can be shared easily. In an article for InMoment.com, Mike contrasts this with "CX integration," which emphasizes:

> The interoperability of software solutions. This involves integrating various tools and platforms to streamline processes, automate workflows, and enhance overall efficiency in delivering exceptional customer experiences. In essence, integrated CX is about centralizing customer data for a unified view, while CX integrations focus on the integration of diverse software tools to enhance the capabilities of the customer experience.[10]

Within One Medical, the centralized and electronic health record (EHR) exemplifies "integrated patient experience." The EHR unifies clinical data from various sources (primary and virtual care team notes, lab results, prescriptions, etc.) in an "accessible repository" that offers a holistic view of the patient's journey. While that internally developed patient health record is easily accessible by relevant One Medical providers, it requires "CX integration" to ensure needed health information is shared with healthcare partners outside of One Medical. CX integrations are also required to guide information flow back to One Medical, streamline referrals to specialists, and align workflows.

Amir Dan Rubin noted that experience designers had to create these CX integrations to accommodate One Medical's many healthcare partners. Amir shares: "On a geographic basis, our team has likely integrated with more healthcare organizations than any other company. Our strategy has always been to help our members by breaking down unnecessary information silos within One Medical and across partnership networks."

To illustrate the magnitude of integration challenges, One Medical's former Chief Technology Officer, Stuart Parmenter, explained how technology tools were designed organically to maximize coordination across One Medical.

> We've built our app and electronic health record (EHR) by iterating on workflows like how our providers prescribe medications or send referrals. We also automated functions like sending a task through our app when a member is due for a health screen and simultaneously notifying their primary care provider. Our EHR makes work easier for our providers, such as checking for medication interactions and addressing regulatory and compliance issues in areas like prescribing controlled substances. It also ensures an integrated patient experience—no matter who cares for them at One Medical.

The care journey of a patient, whom I will call Paula, demonstrates the importance of seamless integration across One Medical, which is supported by the company's care routing system and proprietary EHR. For context, Paula, a 24-year-old woman, was experiencing considerable aches and pains, which prompted a friend to suggest she check out One Medical. Although Paula lived in the San Francisco area, she scheduled a virtual visit while traveling in New York. Andrew Diamond, One Medical's Chief Medical Officer, practices in San Francisco and is also licensed in New York. Andrew had a cancellation at the time Paula requested a virtual appointment, so she was routed to him. Andrew notes, "Our technology is remarkable at managing workflows, patient needs, and licensing requirements, and it enabled me to be available when she needed me." Based on Paula's symptoms (various aches and pains with some swelling), Andrew suspected that she might have rheumatoid arthritis and ordered blood tests through the patient's EHR. According to Andrew, Paula:

> . . . walked to a nearby One Medical office in New York and had her blood drawn. Within 24 hours, I was notified through her health record that her blood results supported a rheumatoid arthritis diagnosis. I contacted her through her app, and we repeated the tests while she was still in New York. Since those results aligned with her prior labs, I began a course of treatment while arranging an appointment for her with a rheumatologist in San Francisco.
>
> Her rheumatology appointment occurred shortly after her return to San Francisco. In the brief period before her return, she was on medication designed to help her feel better faster and prevent long-term damage. For this type of care to occur, a lot of One Medical technology was operating in the background.

While One Medical's proprietary EHR and app provide "integrated care benefits" for One Medical members and providers, they pose challenges when working with healthcare partners outside of One Medical. Stuart Parmenter explains:

> Data interoperability across the healthcare ecosystem starts with ensuring everyone's data is secure and private. So, we invest a lot of time, money, and effort in security. We then focus on processes like getting new patient information, sending referrals, receiving records, and synchronizing vaccine records to state registries. Most hospitals have purchased health record systems like Epic or Cerner, built to support specialties in their network, not to integrate with an EHR like ours. So, we tirelessly work with our partners to ensure our systems communicate with each other in the

right ways and at the right times in the service of our members, partners, and providers.

Failing to work through breakdowns in healthcare interoperability inconveniences patients and providers and negatively affects patient care coordination. In a paper presented at the Hawaii International Conference on System Sciences, Susan Sherer, Chad Meyerhoefer, and Donald Levick shared:

> A landmark 1999 Institute of Medicine (IOM) report established lack of care coordination as a costly problem in the U.S. . . . Subsequent studies reported that the consequences might be more severe than the IOM's original assessment. A 2010 federal report projected that 15,000 Medicare patients every month suffered such serious harm in the hospital that it contributed to their deaths . . . And this is not just a U.S. issue: medical errors, and lack of coordination were found to be pervasive in five highly industrialized countries, including Australia, Canada, New Zealand, the UK, and the U.S.[11]

While coordination breakdowns in healthcare have life-or-death consequences, most businesses face mission-critical challenges in addressing interdepartmental silos and partnership misalignment. Based on the approach taken by One Medical and other clients, here are steps to increase interoperability across your departments and effectively integrate with business partners:

- **Identify and consistently communicate the benefits of interoperability**—These benefits might include increasing employee and customer safety, improving customer access, reducing costs, or strengthening partnerships.
- **Work with departments or partners to define shared goals and the scope of interoperability efforts**—Define the objectives of streamlined collaboration (e.g., improved data sharing, enhanced

decision-making, and increased efficiency). Identify the degree to which departments or businesses should optimally connect.

- **Assess the current state of integration**—Conduct process and technology audits that assess IT infrastructure, data formats, existing software, workflows, redundancies, and gaps.

- **Establish protocols and standards**—Consider legal and regulatory compliance requirements. Standardize application programming interfaces (APIs) and communication protocols. Adopt industry formats and standards (e.g., JSON, XML, or healthcare's HL7).

- **Create integrated technology solutions and interoperable processes**—Leverage cloud solutions that promote flexibility and scalability and consider enterprise service bus (ESB) technologies that connect disparate systems. Implement automated workflows and design processes that ensure interdepartmental or cross-business interactions.

- **Deploy effective change management**—Most change management initiatives fail either due to a lack of strategy or poor execution of that strategy. Consider using a change management framework like **Kotter's 8-step process**, which outlines the following approach:

1. Create a sense of urgency
2. Build a guiding coalition
3. Form a strategic vision
4. Enlist a volunteer army
5. Enable action by removing barriers
6. Generate short-term wins
7. Sustain acceleration
8. Institute change

 (*For more on this change management approach developed by Harvard Business School professor John Kotter, visit kotterinc.com*)

- **Conduct relevant training**—Train team members on the skills needed to ensure seamless integration.

- **Create a governance framework**—Identify who will oversee the interoperability process, create security and data access policies, and monitor compliance.
- **Continually assess and adapt**—Regularly review the performance of integrated systems and processes. Leverage emerging technologies to streamline collaboration further.

Allison Kroll, Senior Director of Product Management at One Medical, explains that interoperability challenges require technological and human-centered design elements.

One of the biggest complaints One Medical had when I joined the company in 2018 was that customers felt like we were entering a dark forest anytime we sent them outside of our four walls for specialty care or additional clinical services. We approached that complaint by asking how we can think about this from a technology and human-centric design perspective. How can we work on technological interoperability and also address how patients feel about the referral process? There were a lot of components to consider, like making sure that when we sent referrals, we prepared the specialist to receive the patient, listened to specialists to understand their processes for actually getting the patient in the door, and ensured that when our member followed up with our One Medical clinician, that provider knew what happened during the member's visit with the specialist. This was particularly challenging because business models outside One Medical didn't necessarily incentivize a seamless experience.

In addition to spending considerable time observing and talking to members, One Medical providers, and specialists, Allison emphasized the importance of fostering human connections to facilitate the referral process.

Our clinical operations teams invest in social events between specialists and One Medical providers because relationships matter.

As we establish a relationship with new health systems, we not only design technology to transfer information seamlessly but also design opportunities for providers and specialists to spend time together and get to know each other. Similarly, we foster interactions between our operations teams and partners to understand how partners accept referrals. How do they do scheduling? How do they conduct patient outreach? This work helps us set proper expectations and support our members throughout the process.

At One Medical, improving interoperability and reducing effort benefits everyone in the service ecosystem. Allison shares:

We want to meet our network partners where they are and design to a standard that works best for our members, partners, and team members. On the One Medical side, we want to free clinicians to practice at the top of their license and ensure our support teams do purposeful work. For example, a member support specialist (MSS) messaged me not long ago, saying, "I've got a patient sitting with me who completed a scan and wants me to call the imaging center to have them fax the record to us." That MSS and a colleague chased down the record; one called the center and waited on hold for seven minutes, and the other logged into the imaging center's portal and searched for the record. Between the two, they found the scan in the third-party portal, downloaded it, uploaded it to our EHR, and tagged it for the provider's review. Through their concerted efforts, they got the information to our clinician. Fast-forward to today, where information comes into our data browser, and our teams conduct real-time queries for any result for that patient across a broad clinical data network. That's a win for our members, support teams, clinicians, and network partners.

Similarly, Kyle Munkittrick, Group Product Manager, describes a large design project related to the member front-desk check-in process that produced a win-win:

A spaghetti diagram showed that during the patient check-in process, a member support specialist (MSS) had to look at seven or eight screens and click something like 60 times. That was manually challenging and also affected their ability to greet patients effectively. Our goals were to reduce screens and clicks while enabling the MSS to spend most of their time looking at and chatting with patients as they come in. Ideally, they would spend only a few seconds looking at their screen—reversing the ratio from 10% patient 90% screen to 90% patient and 10% screen.

Staff Product Designer KP Pelleg suggests that projects like the one described by Kyle also produce an additional win for design team members:

I joined One Medical to contribute to our company's transformative and compassionate care mission. Our design teams feel a sense of fulfillment when we contribute to making healthcare more personal or navigable. We've all experienced pain during our healthcare journeys, and it is rewarding to play a part in alleviating some of that pain and infusing more humanity into the system.

## DESIGNING FOR CUSTOMER EMPOWERMENT

Given rapid technology breakthroughs, human-centered and technology-powered design often gives customers options between self-service or service by others. In healthcare, this typically involves providing patients with information that enables them to either self-treat or determine the urgency of professional care they should seek. A US-based study conducted by the Weber Shandwick agency in partnership with KRC Research suggests that 81% of Americans seek health information at least once a year, and 73% turn to the internet for that information.[12]

Online information seeking leads people to self-diagnose physical and emotional disorders, but the information they rely on isn't necessarily accurate. A 2023 study published in the *Journal of Medical Internet Research* looked at the potential of the AI platform ChatGPT as a self-diagnostic tool for common orthopedic diseases. Those researchers concluded that ChatGPT's reproducibility and accuracy in diagnosing the conditions were inconsistent. "Only a few answers were accompanied by a strong recommendation to seek medical attention according to our study standards. Although ChatGPT could serve as a potential first step in accessing care, we found variability in accurate self-diagnosis. Given the risk of harm with self-diagnosis without medical follow-up, it would be prudent for a [natural language processor] NLP to include clear language alerting patients to seek expert medical opinions."[13] Similarly, research published in *The Canadian Journal of Psychiatry* showed that 52% of TikTok videos about attention deficit hyperactivity disorder (ADHD) were misleading, and the researchers encouraged clinicians to "be aware of the widespread dissemination of health misinformation on social media platforms and its potential impact on clinical care."[14]

The possible negative impact of inaccurate online content includes having people experience needless fear, engage in dangerous home remedies, or delay appropriate care. However, accurate self-help content also has the potential to empower patients to improve their health and well-being. This potential has led to a proliferation of digital health apps. Emily May, a research analyst for the Deloitte Centre for Health Solutions, notes:

> In 2020, more than 90,000 new digital health applications (apps) were added to app stores, more than 250 new apps on average, every day . . . Digital health apps range from providing a platform for services such as virtual GP appointments and chronic disease management to consumer health apps that help people manage their own health through tracking daily steps and accessing exercise and nutrition programmes . . . Health apps are increasingly focused on health condition management rather than wellness management (the proportion of such apps has grown from 28 percent in 2015 to 47 percent in 2020). Mental health (MH), diabetes, and cardiovascular disease-related apps accounting for almost half of disease-specific apps. Indeed, regulated, evidence-based, MH health apps not only improve access to advice and support, but can clinically reduce symptoms of anxiety and depression.[15]

Emily also reported that 88% of digital health applications had the potential to collect and potentially share user data.

One Medical has built features into its membership app beyond appointment setting, virtual visits, and provider communication. In keeping with "self-service" and "digital health," designers have crafted the app to provide accurate health content that empowers healthy choices. For example, let's assume you are a One Medical member experiencing new symptoms and want to determine your best course of care. You open your One Medical app, click the "Treat Me Now" button, and search for your condition from a list of common disorders like:

- Acid Reflux
- Acne
- Athlete's Foot
- Bug Bites
- Cold Sores (Oral Herpes)
- Constipation
- Dandruff
- Eye Redness
- Lice
- Nausea, Vomiting, and Diarrhea
- Seasonal Allergies

Since you have upper respiratory symptoms, you click on Cold, Flu, or COVID-19 and are asked to confirm your location if you need a virtual appointment with a clinician licensed in that state. You are then advised that if you have any of these symptoms:

- Wheezing or difficulty speaking without getting winded
- Severe or persistent chest pain or pressure
- Fever greater than 103°F
- Severe dizziness, confusion, or fainting

you should request a video chat "to expedite care."

If you don't have those symptoms, you will be prompted to provide information like the date of symptom onset, whether you've been recently tested for COVID-19, current symptoms, other health-related questions (e.g., past diagnoses of asthma, COPD, congestive heart failure), and your recent use of prescription or over-the-counter medications. You will then be prompted to verify medication allergies and pharmacy information. At the end of the questionnaire, you are advised to "Hang tight! Our medical team is reviewing your request and will message you with your treatment plan, including any next steps." You are also given a reasonable time by which you should expect that response. Within hours, you'll have a treatment plan that may include how to address the issue (through self-care or other interventions) and when to engage a healthcare professional (virtually or in person).

The "Treat Me Now" resource is an example of human-centered and technology-aided design at its best. Members leverage technology (their app) to learn about and determine the acuity of symptoms. Depending upon condition severity, they are empowered to follow a personalized treatment plan sent to them via the app, seek out immediate virtual care (even if they are traveling out of state), or set a same-day or future appointment (virtually or in person) with their primary care provider. If an urgent virtual care appointment and prescriptions are needed, those prescriptions are directed to a convenient pharmacy.

---

**QUICK CHECKUP**

How have you integrated technology and human-service delivery to give customers options for self-service or service by others?

---

While our focus has been on general design principles and how One Medical has deployed "good design" to create breakthrough technology solutions, streamline interoperability, and foster digital health, chapter 6 will examine how One Medical designs innovative programs and services in pediatrics and mental health. For now, let's examine how functional design goes beyond technology by exploring how One Medical designed the physical environment where members receive care.

## DESIGNING PHYSICAL SPACES

Earlier in this chapter, we highlighted how "pain" moments forge memories for customers. When it comes to healthcare, an all-too-common pain moment is sitting in a clinic waiting room. The Healthcare Pain Index, a report by the experience management company Qualtrics, looks at negative experiences or pain points across primary care, urgent care, and emergency room visits. According to that index:

> In 7 out of 11 rankings, unpleasant waiting areas was the most cited reason patients would not return to a specific facility. Beyond returning to that specific facility in the future, the quality of the waiting room experience factors into one's overall satisfaction with a healthcare visit. Patients who found the waiting room unpleasant at the ER on their last visit were 9X more likely to be dissatisfied with their overall experience. The number was 5X more for primary care patients and 4X more likely for urgent care.[16]

Across all settings, unpleasant waiting areas were reportedly more dissatisfying than long wait times.

Dr. Tom Lee prioritized a positive arrival experience from the launch of One Medical. Experts described early One Medical offices as welcoming, accessible, and personalized. Accordingly, a design firm suggested that the "materials, forms, textures, and details" of One Medical clinics "conspire to create a striking yet comfortable environment."[17] By 2018, however, One Medical needed to create greater consistency and scalability in its office design, so One Medical leaders turned to Laura Harsch.

Laura, One Medical's Senior Director of Design, gained extensive retail design experience from multiple roles at brands like Urban Outfitters and Macy's. Before joining One Medical, Laura was Macy's Vice President of

Branded Environments—Shop Design and Development. Laura explains the strengths and opportunities she faced upon arrival.

Before 2018, all of our offices were unique, and members who regularly visited multiple offices told us they liked the variety and the sense of warmth and hospitality. None of our offices were sterile or cold, with 100 chairs lined up, ready to be hosed down.

However, when I came on board, our growth goals required that we find efficiencies of scale and develop standards for our staff. We didn't want to lose the sense of uniqueness, so we worked with the marketing team to ensure clear brand differentiation that would guide three scalable office designs we called Mind, Body, and Spirit.

Mind is a little more traditional. It is perfect for interesting spaces with history, like residential areas in San Francisco or an area like Chelsea in New York.

Body is utilized in offices in newer buildings where the space might be somewhat plain or where we are the first tenant. So, the Body design provides more architectural interest.

Spirit works well in spaces with lots of windows or natural light. It is more pseudo-Scandinavian, where the colors and textures come more from the materials than anything we add.

All three are visually engaging and create a sense of familiarity and comfort. They are not overly contemporary or traditional, and they each have a bit of whimsy. We are very serious about the care we provide, but we want our spaces to have an edge of fun.

Mind, Body, and Spirit are aesthetically pleasing spaces for members to be welcomed and receive care. They are also warm and uplifting environments for clinic staff. These designs are scalable and evolve to accommodate One Medical's Amazon-fueled growth. Laura notes:

Historically, we've looked for real estate in retail environments rather than medical office buildings, so an office visit fits easily with where our members are having lunch, shopping, or shuttling their children. We will continue to evolve designs around the function of the space to accommodate the changing needs of our teams and members. Because the easier it is for our team to work efficiently in an environment, the easier it will be for our members to get their needs met well.

*(See below for examples of One Medical reception and exam room design.)*

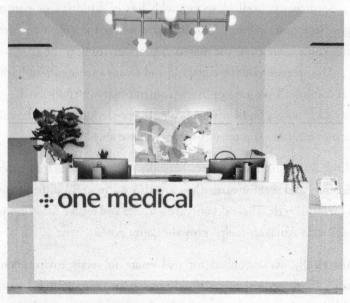

Amir Dan Rubin noted that office standardization helped accelerate One Medical's growth: "When I started in 2017, it took us several months to open a clinic after construction. Our three clinic models (Mind, Spirit, and Body) brought those openings down to days, which, in turn, produced substantial savings for us."

Before we close the chapter with a couple of patient stories that demonstrate One Medical's effective design approach, let's look at how you can apply lessons from One Medical to ensure you are Winning Through People & Technology.

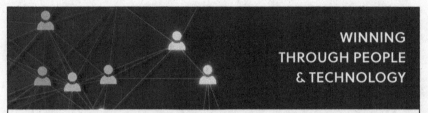

## WINNING THROUGH PEOPLE & TECHNOLOGY

1. How easy is it for your customers/members/patients/guests to get their needs met from your department or organization?

2. Are you measuring customer effort? If so, how does that metric correlate with repeat business and future spending? How will you begin to assess customer effort if you aren't measuring it?

3. What interoperability challenges and opportunities are you facing across your organization and between your organization and business partners?

4. What are your departmental or organizational strengths and weaknesses related to each of these components of successful interoperability?

    a. Identifying and communicating the benefits of interoperability

    b. Defining shared goals and the scope of interoperability efforts

    c. Accessing the current state of integration

    d. Establishing protocols and standards

    e. Creating integrated technology solutions and interoperable processes

    f. Deploying effective change management

g.   Conducting relevant training

h.   Creating a governance framework

i.   Continually assessing and adapting

What might you do to leverage your operability strengths and mitigate weaknesses?

5.   How holistic is your design approach? Are you designing to remove pain points and enhance positively memorable online and offline experiences? Think of examples where you are succeeding and opportunities for improvement.

## HUMAN-CENTERED AND TECHNOLOGY-POWERED DESIGN IN ACTION

To appreciate how One Medical's design approach comes to life, let's explore the experiences of two members. I will call them James and Anthony. In 2011, James was a young, single professional living and working in the Washington, DC, area when he heard about One Medical. While James was interested in a company that was purportedly tech-forward, he was also worried that high-tech might result in a low-touch experience. James notes, "I was used to healthcare being delivered by a kindly older person who would poke and prod me when I occasionally got sick. For me, apps had a place in impersonal service situations like Uber, but how would this translate to personal care associated with yearly exams or receiving injections? Despite my reservations, I tried One Medical hoping to experience increased convenience and flexibility without compromising personal care."

Roughly 13 years later, James remains a One Medical brand advocate who praises the relationship he formed with his primary care provider, One Medical's curated digital health content, and the ease by which he can schedule or engage care with his primary provider or other clinicians. "For a small membership fee, I've built a strong bond with my holistic primary care provider and can get same- or next-day appointments. If I don't need to see my physician, I can receive care from other One Medical providers or drop in for labs at convenient and beautiful locations near where I work. My primary care physician knows me well and helps me navigate anxieties that come from my researching symptoms like weakness in my left arm. My provider calms me. She helps me get to specialists while maintaining an optimistic yet realistic perspective pending a diagnosis and treatment plan."

Similarly, Anthony, a technology engineer based in San Francisco, notes, "One Medical has designed a tech-savvy experience that addresses many of the administrative inefficiencies in healthcare. It appeals to Millennials like me and is a must-have employee perk for technology companies in the San Francisco Bay area. The simplicity of technology design also has my seventy-year-old mother-in-law praising the app." Anthony also acknowledges that One Medical's "app isn't perfect. For example, when setting up an account for my daughter, I needed to provide an email address—which she didn't have. So, I had to create a Google account for her. Those issues are minor but speak to the challenges of designing technology. Ultimately, I hope more businesses—in healthcare and other sectors—will increase customer ease like One Medical." Since the time Anthony opened his daughter's account, One Medical has improved the experience so a parent can create child accounts under their account.

In addition to the digital experience, Anthony emphasizes One Medical's in-person experience and human-centered culture: "historically, going to a doctor's office was unpleasant. However, One Medical clinics don't look like doctors' offices. They are designed with attention to detail, from the types of seats to color patterns. One Medical's physical environment is gorgeous, welcoming, and relaxing, and staff members enhance those qualities. I don't know how they select their teams, but the receptionists, phlebotomists, and providers are clinically exceptional and remarkably skilled at providing care at the highest levels of hospitality."

From the perspectives of James, Anthony, other loyal members, healthcare analysts, and experience designers, One Medical team members innovate human-centered and technology-powered solutions. In the next chapter, we will see how One Medical leaders ensure those solutions are consistently delivered. Former Apple CEO Steve Jobs emphasized the importance of execution in relation to creativity and design by noting, "Ideas are worth nothing unless executed. They are just a multiplier. Execution is worth millions."[18]

Before we look at how One Medical elevates design through execution, let's take a moment to look at this chapter's Transformational Lessons.

## TRANSFORMATIONAL LESSONS

- Albert Einstein said, "The best design is the simplest one that works." Former IDEO CEO Tim Brown believes, "Where you innovate, how you innovate, and what you innovate are design problems." The former president of IBM, Thomas J. Watson Jr., suggested, "Good design is good business."
- Design thinking typically involves a circular, five-phase process: (1) empathize, (2) define, (3) ideate, (4) prototype, and (5) test.
- Personas (fictional characters created from customer segmentation research) help humanize problem statements.
- A persona typically reflects a group's demographics (general characteristics like gender, age, and income), psychographics (interests, attitudes, values, opinions, and lifestyles), experiences, needs, goals, and behaviors.
- Delivering your brand's differentiating elements by designing experiences that leverage technology, products, processes, and people is essential.
- Penchansky and Thomas's access model focuses on five aspects: accessibility, availability, acceptance, affordability, and adequacy or accommodation.
- According to behavioral economists, memorable moments of truth include arrivals, transitions, pain, peaks, and endings.
- Journey mapping provides a longitudinal view of touchpoints across the journey of stakeholders (e.g., team members, customers, and partners).

- In the *Harvard Business Review* article "Stop Trying to Delight Your Customers," Dixon, Freeman, and Toman warn against having team members try to exceed customer expectations due to team confusion, higher costs, and wasted effort. Instead, they recommend designing for customer ease.
- Customer experience (CX) writer Mike Henry distinguishes between "integrated customer experiences" and "CX integrations." Integrated customer experience involves destroying data silos and bringing together diverse customer data into a centralized location. CX integration focuses on the interoperability of software solutions.
- Kotter's eight steps to change management are: (1) create a sense of urgency, (2) build a guiding coalition, (3) form a strategic vision, (4) enlist a volunteer army, (5) enable action by removing barriers, (6) generate short-term wins, (7) sustain acceleration, and (8) institute change.
- Given rapid technology breakthroughs, human-centered and technology-powered design typically seeks to give customers options between self-service or service by others.
- Good design requires a focus on more than technology. It must include an appreciation for both the online and offline experience.
- According to Steve Jobs, "Ideas are worth nothing unless executed. They are just a multiplier. Execution is worth millions."

## CHAPTER 5

# Executing Innovative Solutions

*Ideation without execution is delusion.*

*Robin Sharma, leadership author*
*and consultant[1]*

In their book, *Execution: The Discipline of Getting Things Done*, former Chairman and CEO of Honeywell International, Larry Bossidy, and management consultant Ram Charan provide key insights on business execution. From their perspective, execution is:

1. the primary reason companies underperform;
2. the gap between the aspirations of leaders and actual organizational capacity;
3. a fundamental part of business strategy;
4. the quintessential job of leaders;
5. a methodical approach for understanding your business, people, and environment; and

6. "a system for getting things done through questioning, analysis, and follow-through. A discipline for meshing strategy with reality, aligning people with goals, and achieving the results promised."

This chapter will broadly explore operating and performance management systems and examine how One Medical leaders drive consistency through the One Medical Performance System (TOPS). We will also look at a One Medical interactional template (C-I-CARE) that fuels consistency and quality improvements. Before I get into the nuances of TOPS (e.g., strategic alignment, continuous improvements, and active daily management), let's review the differences, similarities, and benefits of operating and performance management systems.

## OPERATING VS. PERFORMANCE MANAGEMENT SYSTEMS

Since One Medical's TOPS program is a hybrid operating system and performance management system, it's worthwhile to review how each of these frameworks can address the execution gaps spotlighted by Bossidy and Charan. Generally speaking, business operating systems assist with managing day-to-day activities required to meet business objectives. These systems comprise planning resources, procedures, processes, and monitoring tools that guide resource allocation, workflows, and continuous improvement.

Entrepreneur and business author Gino Wickman has popularized his Entrepreneurial Operating System (EOS) in a series of books, including *What the Heck Is EOS?* and *Traction*. Gino views operating systems as having six parts—vision, people, data, issues, process, and traction. Gino explains the importance of an operating system by noting:

You must have one abiding vision, one voice, one culture, and one operating system. This includes a uniform approach to how you meet, how you set priorities, how you plan and set your vision, the terminology you use, and the way you communicate with employees. Just as a computer program is made up of components that organize activity and various data into a system that enables its users to be more productive, [an operating system] does the same for a business.[2]

Like *operating systems, performance management systems seek to increase efficiency and align behavior with organizational goals.* However, performance management systems focus more on individual and team performance than a broader organizational framework. In a 2024 article for McKinsey.com, Amaia Noguera Lasa, Andrea Pedroni, Asmus Komm, and Simon Gallot Lavallée suggest performance management systems are:

Designed to help people get better in their work, and they offer clarity in career development and professional performance. And then there's the big picture: companies that focus on their people's performance are 4.2 times more likely to outperform their peers, realizing an average 30 percent higher revenue growth and experiencing attrition five percentage points lower . . . Companies that focus on their people and organizational health also reap dividends in culture, collaboration, and innovation—as well as sustained competitive performance.[3]

Effective performance management systems help employees grow and develop by establishing actionable goals and providing consistent feedback. Unlike annual performance evaluations, employee performance management requires regular, dynamic feedback to facilitate growth and goal attainment.

As alluded to earlier, the One Medical Performance System combines aspects of an operating framework (organizational infrastructure) and a performance management (individual and team-focused) approach. TOPS is supported by C-I-CARE (connect, introduce, communicate, ask, respond, exit—an ethos that guides all decisions across member, colleague, and client touchpoints) and built on three pillars:

1. strategic alignment and deployment
2. continuous improvement and innovation
3. active daily management

*(See figure below.)*

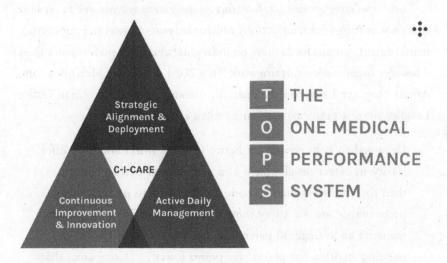

Historically, leaders at One Medical have used TOPS to ensure everyone works "together to create consistently compassionate, respectful, delightful member and team experiences." Jose Gutierrez, One Medical's Vice President of Performance Excellence, notes:

> I get the privilege of overseeing the programmatic efforts related to TOPS, and we think about it in three different parts. (1) How do we help the organization stay strategically aligned with our highest priorities and goals? (2) How do we manage to those goals annually, quarterly, monthly, weekly, and daily? That includes everything from what we measure to the mechanisms we use to gain leverage and create pathways for escalation. (3) How do we provide a system for improvement so that we can solve and mitigate root causes? These three elements are the pillars of our performance system.

## A DEEPER LOOK INTO THE PILLARS

At One Medical, **strategic alignment and deployment** involve setting goals (in keeping with One Medical's mission and DNA) and activating those goals by setting priorities and performance objectives for everyone. At the executive level, senior leaders set strategic direction with input from team members and communicate those goals throughout the organization. Managers and directors then translate the strategic direction into tactical goals, initiatives, and metrics to measure progress. Ultimately, team members understand their priorities and how they contribute to their team and company goals.

One Medical's **continuous improvement and innovation** involve tools and processes for constantly enhancing the value that team members provide to one another and other stakeholders. One Medical is grounded in Lean Six Sigma approaches (discussed more just ahead), uses Gemba walks (where leaders observe and explore workflow tasks), and deploys a process improvement approach called C-I-CARE rounds (part of a broader C-I-CARE interactional and decision-making framework). Finally, **active daily management** involves enterprise-wide, divisional, regional, and office-level alignment meetings, one-on-one coaching, and daily huddles. Let's dive deeper into the key components of the One Medical Performance System (TOPS).

## STRATEGIC ALIGNMENT

At One Medical, all strategies must align with the company's mission:

*To transform healthcare for all through a human-centered,
technology-powered model, delighting millions of members
with better health and care while reducing total costs.*

Essentially, strategic options are assessed by questions like: Is this idea human-centered? Are we effectively leveraging technology? Will it result in an emotionally positive experience? How will this scale and will it reduce cost?

In keeping with One Medical's Lean Six Sigma foundation, one of the tools leaders use to craft strategy is the A3. The A3 was developed as part of Toyota's lean manufacturing model to foster collaboration and effective problem resolution, and its name comes from the size of the single sheet of paper used as a template for the process. The A3 is an effective tool for analyzing problems, documenting findings, and regularly learning and iterating solutions. Leaders at One Medical use the A3 to answer the question: "Where do we want to take One Medical in the near future?" They view the A3 as providing a comprehensive review of an issue's context and background. It is also viewed as a constructive way to identify possible root causes of a problem—allowing One Medical to use a scientific method to identify gaps, outline ideas, plan, and set goals throughout the problem-solving process. According to One Medical leaders, the A3 also "helps tell the strategy 'story' that gets us from where we are today to where we want to go." *(See a One Medical A3 template in figure below.)*

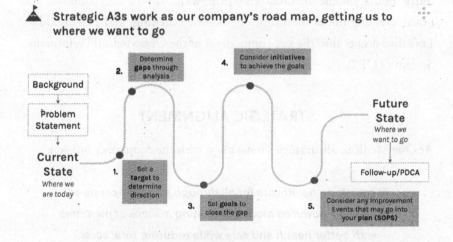

Strategic A3s work as our company's road map, getting us to where we want to go

A3s, in conjunction with One Medical's mission and key objectives, are supplemented with bidirectional, horizontal, and vertical input to create strategic operating plans (SOPs). These plans are clearly defined, measurable, and time-bound performance expectations and answer the question: "How will we get to our desired destinations efficiently?"

SOPs, in turn, guide meetings where team members align and reflect on how they can apply scientific problem-solving to ensure individual and team-based goal-setting and actions that support organizational goals. For example, assume a One Medical strategic goal is to continue to improve world-class patient experience scores as measured by the Net Promoter Score. For administrative team members in a One Medical clinic, this might translate to increasing the first-time resolution of billing inquiries and looking for ways they can individually and collectively drive problem resolution.

## VALUE STREAM IMPROVEMENTS

Will Kimbrough, MD, One Medical's Vice President of Strategic Clinical Services and clinician, notes, "Lean Six Sigma and value stream improvements are baked into our day-to-day mindset. Early on, we did a lot of kaizen events and continue to go to Gemba."

> **QUICK CHECKUP**
>
> What value stream improvement processes are "baked into" your organization's "day-to-day mindset"?

Lean Six Sigma methodology is a managerial framework that blends Lean process improvement (based on *kaizen*, a lean manufacturing model developed over decades and deployed by Toyota in the 1960s) and Six Sigma methodology (developed by Motorola in 1986). Some of the basics of kaizen (which translates from Japanese to mean "change for the better") are its five principles and three Mu, as detailed below.

Kaizen's five core principles drive "pure improvement" for everyone, everywhere, every day by:

1. **Knowing your customer**—Understanding them so you can enhance their experience.
2. **Letting it flow**—Ensuring everyone in your organization is targeting "zero waste."
3. **Being transparent**—Guiding through the use of tangible and visible data.
4. **Empowering people**—Setting clear goals for everyone in the organization.
5. **Going to Gemba**—Spending time and attention at Gemba (which translates from Japanese to the "actual place" where things happen and where value is created).

The three Mu focus on elements of quality loss:

- **Muda**—Waste
- **Mira**—Unevenness or irregularity
- **Muri**—Overburden or excessiveness

Many commonly used business concepts like "internal customer" come from kaizen. For example, a kaizen concept, *adon* (the Japanese word for lamp), resulted in green, yellow, and red indicator "lamps" on performance dashboards. As lean manufacturing processes expanded to non-manufacturing settings, lean practitioners focus primarily on removing inefficiency or waste (*muda*).

Six Sigma is a compatible process improvement methodology that seeks to identify and fix the root cause of quality defects or errors. The Six Sigma approach often involves a five-step DMAIC process, which stands for:

- Define
- Measure
- Analyze
- Improve
- Control

With this grounding in Lean Six Sigma methodology, let's examine how One Medical empowers all team members to improve value streams.

## CONTINUOUS IMPROVEMENT AND INNOVATION

Leaders at One Medical suggest that the best member and team experience occurs when everyone in the organization is looking for ways to maximize their "respect for people," "create greater value," and "eliminate waste" (*see figure below*).

 We embrace three core principles to achieve a better member and team member experience

To ensure these outcomes, leaders map value streams (all actions required to deliver products and services to customers) through a six-step process.

1. **Capturing the current state**—This step results in a visual representation showing how products are currently developed or services are being delivered.

2. **Analyzing waste and pain points**—During this phase, team members look for inefficiencies, friction, and stakeholder pain throughout current processes. They define waste as "anything that doesn't add value" and borrow from common types of waste outlined in lean methodologies. One Medical teams specifically look for eight types of waste:

   a. **Overproduction**—Making too much of something or making it too soon.

   b. **Waiting**—When a person or item is ready for the next step but the process isn't ready for them.

c. **Overprocessing**—Unnecessary steps in work processes that don't add value.

d. **Motion**—Unnecessary movement of people or items within a workspace.

e. **Inventory**—Buying or storing products or materials that are not needed at this time.

f. **Defects**—Time and materials spent on something of poor quality that requires fixing.

g. **Transportation**—Moving items, people, or supplies more often or over farther distances than is necessary.

h. **Human potential**—Skills and scope of work malalignment, unused creativity.

3. **Designing the future state**—This step ensures the process doesn't become overly focused on remediating pain to the exclusion of finding new ways to deliver value. This phase results in a future state map that captures optimal and sometimes disruptive ideal processes.

4. **Brainstorming ideas**—During brainstorming, team members are encouraged to reflect and share unfiltered ideas for removing waste, resolving pain, or approximating the ideal future state.

5. **Prioritizing improvements**—During this step, the most actionable ideas from brainstorming are prioritized. Solutions are designed, and the iterative design processes outlined in chapter 4 are tested.

6. **Implementing**—The most value-producing prototypes are deployed in this phase and are refined based on data.

By involving all team members in the value stream improvement process, leaders at One Medical have positioned the organization to execute four overarching quality outcomes for all stakeholders:

- **Patient satisfaction and engagement**—More on this in the context of the Net Promoter System later in this chapter.

- **Improved population health**—Outlined in chapter 3.

- **Cost reductions**—Noted in chapter 3.
- **Team member well-being**—Reviewed in chapter 2.

# ACTIVE DAILY MANAGEMENT

At One Medical, active daily management focuses on helping everyone in the organization visualize performance and involves:

1. Daily and C-I-CARE rounding
2. Huddles with visual management
3. Going to Gemba and standard work
4. Leadership standard work

Let's look at each of these components in some detail.

## 1. Daily and C-I-CARE Rounding

**Daily rounding** requires One Medical leaders to intentionally check in with team members to learn their work status, proactively identify potential problems, and set a plan for the day. During this rounding process, managers and leaders ask questions like:

- How are you feeling about your day?
- What is your priority today? What is worrying you?
- What might cause barriers to flow today?
- Did anything happen yesterday that we didn't anticipate?
- What, if any, were the high-stress incidents in the last 24 hours? Is there anyone we need to debrief?
- Who on the team do you want to recognize or want me to recognize?
- What (if anything) can I do to support you today?

One Medical leaders believe that rounding at the start of the day allows them to assess and anticipate challenges, decreasing "the need for firefighting." It also ensures that deviations from quality standards are remedied quickly.

Director of Model Experience Amy Livingston characterizes this daily rounding as a check-in to ensure:

> We are operationally ready to start the day. Is there unexpected construction on the road in front of the building? If so, the office manager might remind the team about our late patients' standard work so that everybody is poised to empathically and productively assist people who are running late. Daily rounding gets leaders out from their desks to engage all care team members.

In addition to anticipating and addressing issues before they become crises, the team at the global professional services company the Huron Group reports that "when done well," daily managerial rounding leads to enhanced workplace communication and better morale. Specifically, they note:

> Rounding builds increased levels of trust by demonstrating to staff that the organization's leaders are interested in their day-to-day processes and the quality of their work. They also allow employees to build relationships with leaders while leaders learn what is really important to them. By collecting employee suggestions and following up on them, leaders show that they take employee feedback seriously and care about their contributions.[4]

In addition to **daily rounding**, One Medical leaders conduct **C-I-CARE rounds**. Before I explain the C-I-CARE rounding process, let's first look at C-I-CARE in its broader context—C-I-CARE is the "ethos of" TOPS and a unifying interactional framework.

In the late 2000s, I consulted for David Feinberg, MD (then UCLA Health System CEO), and Amir Dan Rubin (then UCLA Health System COO) during the initial development and deployment of C-I-CARE. (I also provided a detailed review of C-I-CARE and C-I-CARE rounding at UCLA's hospitals and specialty clinics for my book *Prescription for Excellence: Leadership Lessons for Creating a World-Class Customer Experience from UCLA Health System*.)

Amir introduced C-I-CARE to Stanford Hospital and clinics as president and chief executive officer. Subsequently, he introduced it to One Medical. C-I-CARE is an evidence-based communication template (similar to healthcare administrator and consultant Quint Studer's AIDET concept, which stands for acknowledge, introduce, duration, explanation, and thank). C-I-CARE is an acronym for (and is explained in One Medical training material as):

- **Connect**—Even the smallest connection—a smile or eye contact— can create a positive, lasting impact. Making connections with our patients, our colleagues, and our business partners creates lasting impressions and an environment that is human-centered and team-based.

- **Introduce**—A good introduction fosters familiarity and ensures a mutual understanding for the purpose and goals for every interaction. Thoughtful introductions build the foundation for trust and collaboration.

- **Communicate**—Communicating encourages understanding and allows people to clarify and anticipate needs and expectations. Explain what you are going to do, and be transparent and clear about what the patient or team member can expect next. When we communicate clearly and with empathy for our listener, we increase understanding and build productive relationships.

- **Ask**—Ask permission and ask questions to demonstrate respect and courteousness. This promotes understanding and a healthy dialogue, because a relationship is about two people in dialogue and not one person in monologue. We build relationships and provide outstanding experiences by inviting others into dialogue with us, supporting and addressing their questions and concerns.

- **Respond**—Responding with anticipation shows respect and attentiveness to the person we're speaking with, driving the conversation forward with meaning and purpose. By listening deeply to the other person's perspective, we're able to gain insight and understanding of their needs and can better tailor our responses to provide the best information. A clear and thoughtful response not only builds trust and shows a commitment to a strong and lasting relationship, but it also cuts down on patient confusion and added work. Anticipating needs and responding with empathy provides the opportunity to share our expertise and create better experiences.

- **Exit**—Exit politely and confidently, and always end with a thank-you to show appreciation. A good exit ensures that we have met or exceeded the expectations of those we care for and support. Behavioral studies have shown one of the most memorable parts of an interaction is the end (it's called the "Peak-End rule"). But all too often we rush through an ending, thinking about the follow-up work we have to do or already looking ahead to our next patient. Giving our patients clarity, warmth, and respect in our exits creates a positive, lasting impression.

For One Medical leaders, C-I-CARE is more than an intentional communication tool. It is a holistic approach to relationship-based care, a strategic framework, a culture-building resource, and a way to conduct team-based rounds. Specific to rounding, C-I-CARE is a filter by which teams across One Medical assess and share findings on strengths and opportunities to improve stakeholder experiences.

In an interview for Stanford Medicine X, Amir Dan Rubin described C-I-CARE rounding:

Managers participate in monthly C-I-CARE rounds, during which they visit both clinical and non-clinical areas across the enterprise to observe and coach employees and provide rewards and recognition. We also speak with patients and their families to learn what's working and where we need to improve, and then report back to the larger group. This feedback loop allows us to monitor our progress and identify new areas in need of attention. The key is to continuously practice and model this behavior so that it becomes woven into the fabric of our culture.

Similarly, Faith Watson, an Arizona-based One Medical Office Manager, notes:

C-I-CARE truly sets One Medical apart from any other company. All One Medical leaders must do formal C-I-CARE rounds at least once a month, but we do them weekly in our region. Before conducting our observations, we connect virtually as a leadership team and then spend an hour observing. Afterward, we discuss positives, opportunities, and best practices.

Amy Livingston, One Medical's Director of Model Experience and Lean Six Sigma Black Belt, explains how the C-I-CARE rounding process results in local and systemic improvements:

After we debrief what we learn from monthly C-I-CARE rounds, we provide a survey tool so participants can identify the next steps or escalations. Usually, we get between 150 and 200 escalations each month. Some of those items are being managed at the office level. For example, if I noticed a piece of paper taped to an office window in an unappealing way, that would be handled at the office level. Other smaller issues must be addressed before they fester into something more significant. This might be the observation of a clunky workflow for patients checking in for appointments without having their insurance cards on file. We track all items on that escalation list and resolve about 75% of them each month, with some issues needing more time to solve.

Before we look at One Medical's processes for huddles, visual management, Going to Gemba, coaching, and responding to member feedback, let's look at how you can apply lessons from One Medical to ensure you are Winning Through People & Technology.

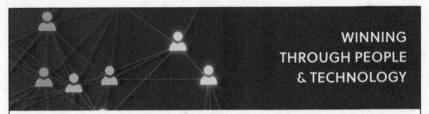

1. Do you agree with Larry Bossidy and Ram Charan that poor execution (not misguided strategy) is the primary reason companies underperform? Also, do you agree that execution is "a system for getting things done through questioning, analysis, and follow-through"? If not, how does your definition of execution differ?

2. Does your organization have an "operating system," a "performance management system," or some combination of both? If so, what is it, and what are its benefits? If not, how might you benefit from implementing elements of an operating or performance management system?

3. Where are your team, department, or organizational strengths and opportunities regarding execution? What can you expressly point to about those strengths and opportunities?

4. What methods do you have in place to ensure leaders intentionally check in with team members to learn their work status, proactively identify potential problems, and set a plan for the day? How well are these methods working, and what gaps exist in these areas?

5. What do you make of One Medical's C-I-CARE concept and C-I-CARE rounds? How might you extrapolate C-I-CARE and C-I-CARE rounds elements for your team, department, or organization?

## 2. Huddles with Visual Management

In the context of active daily management, let's expand beyond "rounding" and focus on daily huddles. At One Medical, huddles are a brief time for team members to connect around a visual management board (in person or virtually). Huddles foster team engagement, information sharing, planning, and collaboration. During One Medical huddles, team members share improvement opportunities, solve problems, make data-driven decisions, and celebrate achievements.

To reinforce the ideas and information provided in these huddles, One Medical presents data visually on an organized "visual management" board. Visual management boards (also referred to as "show boards") are lean tools that include standards (target performance), problems (deviations from the standard), and actions (what needs to be done to meet the standard).

Timothy McLean, the Managing Director of TXM Lean Solutions, suggests a visual management wall should align with the "31-second rule." According to Timothy, when you look at the board:

> In **1 second**, it can tell us if it's normal (everything is fine in the work area), according to the standards (target or plan). The work area should "talk" to you in simple terms. Usually, companies use green to represent good status (e.g., hit the target on time) and use red to represent problem status (e.g., lower than the target, delayed).
>
> In **10 seconds**, it tells us what the problem is, and if it's not normal . . .
>
> In **20 seconds**, it tells us what action is to be taken, who is responsible for this, and what support is needed.[5]

One Medical's Senior Strategic Operations manager, Jenna Killoran, agrees that visual boards should quickly convey performance information, noting:

> Anyone should be able to see what is not working within 30 seconds of looking at the board. For example, our care teams should know if we need better same-day or next-day access so they can immediately focus on increasing it. They should see where they are, where they want to be, and what improvements can or are in place.

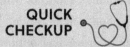

**QUICK CHECKUP**

How do you ensure team members can quickly assess important performance data, expedite solutions, and track resolution?

At One Medical, visual management boards are generally arranged around performance, innovation, and growth—PIG. (*Please see the visual board image below.*)

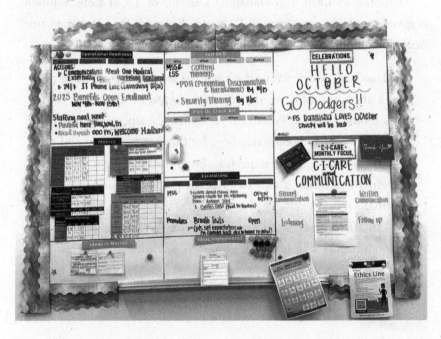

Grant Troyer, a One Medical office manager based in Washington state, explains:

In my offices, we have physical huddle boards in the lunchrooms and designated times to meet there. Virtually, we have a private channel where I recap what we went over in the huddle and provide links. Virtual huddle recaps are an excellent resource for people who are out of the office or want to see what they missed when they return from PTO.

For leaders in my district, our visual boards are standardized, very clean, and precise with action items and announcements, but we can tailor content for each office.

Faith Watson shares the layout of her regions' visual boards:

We track methods, equipment, supplies, performance, completed projects, innovation, announcements, birthdays, celebrations, and key cultural events. Our boards include escalations and "ideas in motion" in a PDCA (Plan, Do, Check, Act) format. We also include C-I-CARE on the board and identify follow-up items.

As needed, issues and concerns raised in an office huddle can escalate quickly at One Medical. Jenna Killoran, Senior Strategic Operations manager, explains:

Our tiered and cascading huddle structure helps us rapidly communicate mission-critical information up and down our organization. That system allows us to solve today's problems today. In our offices, we huddle early in the morning. Those huddles are followed by district, regional, and executive huddles. If operational issues need to be in front of our executives, they will hear them during their midday huddle to fix them immediately. Typically, however, if an office manager can't address an issue (like a patient coming in for an IUD and there aren't any in inventory at that office), the problem is resolved at the district level by having an IUD rushed over from another office before the patient's appointment.

Now that you have a sense of One Medical's cascading huddles and visual management boards, let's consider the more formal way managers oversee work areas, such as Going to Gemba.

## 3. Going to Gemba and Standard Work

As you'll recall, "Gemba" refers to the "actual place"—where things happen and where value is created. Thus, Gemba walks (also referred to as "going and seeing") are a powerful practice utilized for observing work processes, engaging with employees, and identifying opportunities for improvement directly at the source of work. These visits to where work gets done are integral for maintaining open lines of communication between leadership and frontline staff, defining standard work, and creating an environment of continuous improvement and learning. At One Medical, the Gemba walk involves seven actions:

1. Choosing a theme for the visit;
2. Preparing the team that will be visited;
3. Focusing on process observation, not on the people;
4. Ensuring that the visit is conducted where the work is done;
5. Recording observations;
6. Considering if a partner should be included to garner additional observations and insights; and
7. Following up with purposeful action.

During a Gemba walk, One Medical leaders might ask questions like:

- What are you currently working on?
- Is there an established process for this type of work? If not, how would you define the "standard work" (the best practice for getting the work done)?
- Assuming there is standard work, what, if any, problems do you have with the process?
- What are the possible root causes of problems, and how might they be fixed?

At One Medical, Gemba walks and working groups play an important role in creating standards, ensuring those standards are taught to new hires, managing the standards, and continually looking for ways to improve standard work. Jenna Killoran shares:

Those who do the work know how to do it best. In our system, people create and validate standard work specific to their roles. Medical support specialists create standard work for scheduling or conducting a check-in. They validate and publish those standards, and training leads participate in the creation process—so they understand how to communicate those standards to new hires. Gemba walks ensure managers are guiding, supporting, and discussing standard work. Sometimes, those walks result in a manager learning that a team member has a better way of doing something, which gets looped back to our workgroups and results in updated standard work.

Office Manager Faith Watson explains how she uses Gemba walks as both an orientation and process improvement tool:

> While "Going to Gemba" is expected of leaders, I also encourage it as part of onboarding. For example, support specialists might observe the lab, or clinical team members might observe the office team. The goal is to understand other team members' essential roles, see their workflows, and discuss ways to communicate effectively and work well together. When I do my managerial Gemba walks, I look for ways to improve service and efficiency. I use a managerial pre-work tool that ensures I know the standard work I will observe and am in the right mindset. I record my observations and do a short wrap-up with the person I observe. During that debrief, I call attention to the positive things that the person has done and, if needed, offer constructive tweaks. We might also agree to discuss the process in an upcoming coaching session.

## 4. Leadership Standard Work

One Medical managers have standard work expectations and tools to help them manage their workflow. In addition to conducting rounds, leading huddles, creating visual boards, participating in C-I-CARE rounds, and Going to Gemba, a manager's standard work includes coaching and responding to patient feedback from Net Promoter System surveys.

From a coaching perspective, managers must meet regularly with every team member. These sessions systematically ensure regular, constructive interactions between managers and those they support. At the clinic level, One Medical managers often oversee a diverse team (at different levels of tenure and career progression), including Member Support Specialists, Shift Leads, Lab Services Specialists, and Flex Specialists across different offices. This varied team structure necessitates a tailored approach to coaching, customized for the unique needs of each team member. The primary goals of this coaching are to reinforce positive behaviors, provide constructive feedback, and outline development pathways. This proactive engagement helps maintain a motivated team prepared to meet and exceed performance expectations. (*See figure below.*)

Office Manager Grant Troyer shares his "standard work" coaching time commitment, noting:

> I have seven direct reports and manage our laboratory specialists. I partner with another lab support manager on clinical issues and focus primarily on laboratory operations. When people start with us, I schedule an hour weekly for one-on-one coaching to ensure new hires receive the support they need. My standard work expectation for coaching is at least a half hour every two weeks.

### Useful tools and behaviors for implementing TOPS into our daily work

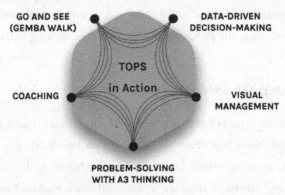

GO AND SEE (GEMBA WALK)

DATA-DRIVEN DECISION-MAKING

TOPS in Action

COACHING

VISUAL MANAGEMENT

PROBLEM-SOLVING WITH A3 THINKING

On a daily basis, the standard work of One Medical clinic managers includes tracking and responding to patient feedback (e.g., responses to formal visit surveys or informal comments on social media platforms). As noted earlier, all members receive a survey through their app after a clinical visit. That survey consists of the following:

1. *How likely is it that you would recommend the provider you saw to a friend or colleague?*
2. *How likely is it that you would recommend One Medical to a friend or colleague?*
3. *If we did not meet your expectations, in what areas could we have improved your experience?*

To understand the manager's role in response to this requested member input, I will provide a quick overview of the Net Promoter Score (NPS). The NPS is a single-question metric used to gauge the emotional engagement and likely repeat business of customers or, in this context, patients/ members. The question initially advocated by Fred Reichheld in a 2003 *Harvard Business Review* article titled "The One Number You Need to Grow" (and later refined and expanded into a comprehensive feedback management system in books like *The Ultimate Question* and *The Ultimate Question 2.0*) asks customers to rate the likelihood that they will recommend a business or service on a 0 to 10 scale with 0 being "not at all likely" and 10 being "extremely likely." In the Net Promoter System, respondents who provide a 9 or 10 rating are viewed as "promoters." Respondents who rate the business or service as a 7 or 8 are called "passives." Individuals whose rating is 6 or less are called "detractors."

The Net Promoter Score is calculated by subtracting the detractors from the promoters and dividing by the total number of respondents. The resulting number, which can range from –100 (all detractors and no passives or promoters) to 100 (all promoters and no detractors or passives), is used to guide customer experience decisions and benchmark companies within or outside a sector. In healthcare, for example, the Lobbie Institute cites various industry benchmarking studies indicating scores "between +38 and +58 and can vary by specialty, facility type, market, etc. Bain & Company (the creators of NPS) note that a good NPS score is 0 and above.

Above 50 is excellent, and above 80 is world-class."[6] One Medical consistently maintains an NPS of 90 plus.

In healthcare, NPS categorizations correlate with important clinical outcomes. Writing for Experience Benchmarks, Sabrina Tessitore reports:

> The average promoter re-admission rate is 4.7% lower than for detractors.
>
> The average promoter emergency room return rate is 7.7% lower than that of detractors.
>
> The average care compliance is 14.2% higher in promoters than detractors.[7]

Many organizations implementing the NPS have a laser focus on the output score and fail to execute the Net Promoter System. However, One Medical's world-class Net Promoter Scores (90 plus) result from deploying a comprehensive approach that actively monitors member/patient feedback and creates individual, clinic-level, and enterprise-wide improvements based on that feedback. In short, One Medical managers are responsible for tracking, communicating with patients, and engaging team members in improvement discussions. In the Net Promoter System, this is referred to as closing the "inner loop" (working with colleagues to create process improvements) and the "outer loop" (speaking with individual customers in response to their feedback).

Senior Operations Manager Xander Salvador explains his role in this process:

> NPS is part of a core task in a manager's standard work. So, every morning, I check our new surveys, and if we have a passive or detractor, I immediately let them know they are heard. I also tell them I want to help and ask what they need. Additionally, I respond to everyone who provides a comment—whether that comment is complimentary or expressing a need or concern. In addition to resolving issues for the individual, I am looking for root causes, which I address with team members or escalate to organizational process improvements. For example, we might get

an eight based on someone having difficulty parking near one of our clinics.

To reinforce the importance of using the Net Promoter System for experience improvement as opposed to obsessing about the score, Amy Livingston (whose team oversees member experience surveys) notes:

> I've had office managers contact me to see if we could change an NPS score survey because when they followed up with a patient, they told them they must have accidentally marked 1 when they meant to mark 10. We don't change the numbers because it isn't about the score; it's about identifying opportunities for improvement. Those errant scores also blend into the hundreds of promoter surveys our clinics receive each month.

**QUICK CHECKUP**

Does your organization focus on survey *scores* or the *process* needed to use input to drive improvements?

In addition to deploying the Net Promoter System, One Medical also informally listens to customer input. For example, One Medical's Vice President of Performance Excellence Jose Gutierrez reports:

> We want to create a space for members to share their complaints or grievances and we listen for issues on social media. Often, people need to talk about a less-than-ideal experience, and we want to listen. My team triages this feedback, and most of the time, a complaint is resolved during a single interaction or by having their clinician contact them. In situations like billing, a resolution might involve cross-functional team members. When my team engages a member, we always loop in relevant office or clinical team members, letting them know: we just chatted with Joseph, who visited their clinic last week. Here's what Joseph experienced. He is all set,

but we wanted to make sure that you heard the feedback—in case you want to follow up with him. That's how we close the loop on the informal feedback received from specific members and how we use it to decrease the likelihood similar issues will occur.

Before we look at how team members and patients experience One Medical's TOPS program, let's look at how you can apply lessons from One Medical to ensure you are Winning Through People & Technology.

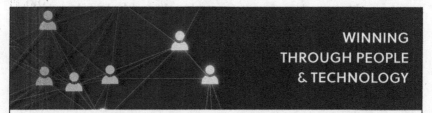

## WINNING THROUGH PEOPLE & TECHNOLOGY

1. Do you provide daily huddles or other processes to ensure daily team, department, or organizational alignment? If so, how do these communication mechanisms affect execution? If not, how might you efficiently deploy these types of approaches?

2. How are you helping your team, department, or organization visualize "Performance, Innovation, and Growth (PIG)"?

3. How consistently do managers go to where the "work gets done" (Go to Gemba) and have process improvement discussions with the team members doing the work?

4. What steps do managers follow to ensure productive dialogue when they engage frontline team members?

5. How do you ensure team members observe and converse about effectively collaborating with individuals in other parts of your organization?

6. How is standard work defined? How is standard work improved?

7. What is expected of managers related to coaching and team member development? How effective is coaching in your organization? How do you know?

8. Do you use the NPS? If so, how effectively do you close the inner and outer feedback loops? Are you consistently performing at "world-class" levels?

## THE IMPACT OF EXECUTION

One Medical's success is a function of designing and executing value. However, Jenna Killoran explains that One Medical's view of value differs from that of many organizations grounded in lean methodologies:

> For us, value equals member satisfaction plus team member well-being minus cost. In many lean organizations, value is simply price minus cost, resulting in a narrower focus on waste and efficiency. However, we take a more holistic view by factoring in team member well-being and satisfaction.

By creating an operating system that focuses on respect, stakeholder value, and waste elimination, leaders at One Medical have sustained "world-class" human experience delivery and positively improved the lives of their team members well beyond the workplace. For example, a Shift Lead in New York City notes: "I have learned how to communicate effectively . . . This company helped me realize the importance of team partnership when it comes to completing projects and assisting with day-to-day tasks. C-I-CARE is not an acronym for just the company but a lifestyle that is embedded in me forever."

Similarly, a phlebotomist and medical assistant from San Francisco describes execution at One Medical as productive, innovative, and adaptive, sharing: "One Medical is an incredible place to work, grow, and find yourself. The company fosters a culture of kindness and development, motivates innovation and progress, and, above all else, a drive to improve the world of healthcare and beyond."

Patients also notice consistent execution and operational excellence, as noted in Yelp and Trustpilot reviews from members like Dipesh and Morlene. Dipesh shares:

> I have seen many doctors in the DC area for annual checkups in the last 7 years. I have probably changed doctors every year due to their inefficient offices, unethical billing practices, or just rude front office staff. One Medical is none of those things . . . Everything ran

on time, offices and exam rooms were large and clean. Even getting blood work done was a snap. The follow-up before and after the visit by the support staff was also top notch. I really think my quest for a primary check-up doctor is over!

Morlene notes:

One Medical has taken the experience of traditional doctor's office visits and flipped it on its head—with waiting rooms that feel like cozy lounges . . . and healthcare practitioners who are completely progressive and open-minded about the holistic care patients need. One Medical brings healthcare into the 21st century. I've seamlessly booked appointments for physicals and PCR tests via their online portal, which is the same place I have communicated with my healthcare professional and where I've received and viewed reports. My visits have started on time and even the sort of questions I was asked about my general health during my appointments revealed a much more nuanced and progressive approach to medicine than I've previously encountered during doctor's visits. I can't say enough how refreshing this is. My nurse was very easy to reach via a message on their online portal. I got a very prompt response when I had an issue with a prescription, and within the hour they were refilling the prescription at the pharmacy I needed. I finally feel heard by my healthcare provider, which I think will have untold benefits on my health in the long run.

Details matter, and so do operational excellence and kindness! By designing and delivering consistent value, One Medical has experienced steady growth. By ensuring people compassionately deliver value, One Medical garners referrals. A member I spoke to, who I'll call John, notes:

I've always appreciated One Medical's technology, efficiency, and consistency. However, ever since I lost a job during the pandemic, I became an advocate who refers One Medical to my friends. The job loss came right as my One Medical membership was up for renewal. I reached out to them amid my uncertainty, and they waived that renewal fee [pursuant to One Medical's financial assistance policy]. It was only a matter of a few months before I was back to work, but that act of kindness, coupled with the quality of their offerings, took me from being an engaged member to a zealot.

Chapters 6 and 7 will explore how One Medical will likely grow exponentially—through program expansion and Amazon's operational expertise.

Before we look at growth from a human-centered and technology-powered perspective, let's take a moment to review this chapter's Transformational Lessons.

## TRANSFORMATIONAL LESSONS

- Robin Sharma said, "Ideation without execution is delusion."
- Business operating and performance management systems seek to increase efficiency and align behavior with organizational goals.
- Gino Wickman's Entrepreneurial Operating System (EOS) has six components: vision, people, data, issues, process, and traction.
- One Medical's combined operating and performance management system is called the One Medical Performance System (TOPS). TOPS is supported by C-I-CARE (an ethos that guides all decisions across member, colleague, and client touchpoints).
- TOPS is built on three pillars: (1) strategic alignment and deployment, (2) continuous improvement and innovation, and (3) active daily management.
- One Medical uses the A3 as part of strategic alignment and deployment. The A3 is an effective tool for comprehensively analyzing problems, documenting findings, and regularly learning and iterating solutions.

- As part of continuous improvement and innovation, One Medical maps value streams through a six-step process: (1) capture the current state, (2) analyze waste and pain points, (3) design the future state, (4) brainstorm ideas, (5) prioritize improvements, and (6) implement.

- As part of active daily management, One Medical deploys (1) daily and C-I-CARE rounding, (2) huddles with visual management, (3) going to Gemba and standard work, and (4) leadership standard work.

- Visual management boards (also referred to as "show boards") are lean tools that include standards (target performance), problems (deviations from the standard), and actions (what needs to be done to meet the standard).

- C-I-CARE is an evidence-based communication template, a unifying interactional framework, and a tool for organizational rounding. C-I-CARE stands for connect, introduce, communicate, ask, respond, exit.

- Gemba walks (also referred to as "Going and Seeing") are powerful for observing work processes, engaging with employees, and identifying opportunities for improvement directly at the source of work.

- At One Medical, Gemba walks play an important role in co-creating standards between managers and team members, ensuring those standards are taught to new hires, managing to the standards, and continually looking for ways to improve standard work.

- One Medical managers are expected to meet regularly with every team member. These sessions systematically ensure regular, constructive interactions between managers and those they support.

- One Medical's sustained world-class NPS scores (90 plus) are the result of closing the "inner loop" (working with colleagues to create process improvements) and the "outer loop" (speaking with individual customers in response to their feedback).

# Sustainable Growth

## CHAPTER 6

# Growth of People and Capacity

*All change is not growth, as all*
*movement is not forward.*

*Ellen Glasgow, Pulitzer*
*Prize–winning novelist[1]*

'm convinced if you want to grow a business (especially one that is human-centered and technology-powered), you need to grow your people first. Through the creativity and passion of your people, you will grow products, services, and brand awareness that fosters sustainability. Put differently, MIT professor Peter Senge, author of *The Fifth Discipline: The Art & Practice of The Learning Organization*, suggests that a learning company "is an organization that is continually expanding its capacity to create its future."[2]

Since labor costs account for up to 70% of a company's operating expenses, successful businesses ensure that human talent is developed in ways that promote organizational performance. Scott Keller and Mary

Meaney (writing for the *McKinsey Quarterly*) indicate that "in highly complex occupations . . . high performers are an astounding 800 percent more productive."[3]

Unfortunately, many companies fail to invest in the developmental resources needed to enhance human performance and retain team members. For example, researchers at Zurich Insurance Company note, "70% of employees report that they don't have mastery of the skills needed to do their jobs . . . [and] 47% of Harvard Business' How We Learn survey participants said they are dissatisfied with their employer's learning and development program."[4] According to a PWC CEO survey, "Eight out of ten CEOs say skill shortages threaten their companies' growth. These shortages are stunting innovation, hurting quality, and limiting the pursuit of market opportunities."[5]

---

**QUICK CHECKUP**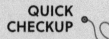

Are skill shortages stunting your organization's innovation, hurting quality, or limiting opportunities?

---

In this chapter, we will explore how One Medical helps its people grow so that the company can expand its offerings and benefit from Amazon's vast resources. We will also examine One Medical's evolving brand strategy and customer segmentation work. In chapter 7, we will examine One Medical's meteoric growth potential in the context of the Amazon partnership and explore the strategic opportunities ahead for Amazon One Medical.

## FORMALIZED LEARNING AND DEVELOPMENT

In chapter 2, we reviewed the emphasis One Medical leaders place on attracting, selecting, and onboarding team members. The preceding chapter also touched on operational coaching, rounding, "Going to Gemba," and other supportive managerial behaviors. Now, let's look at One Medical's longstanding commitment to team member growth and a few of the company's formal learning and development programs.

One Medical's founder and first CEO, Tom Lee, told me, "I have a strong bias for internal development and promotion from within. Developing people builds a stronger culture, fuels growth, and drives sustainability." Subsequent senior leaders have shared Tom's perspective on the importance of growing clinical, frontline, and leadership talent. Former CEO Amir Dan Rubin noted, "We have an obligation to ensure our people maximize their talents and fulfill their purpose. Supporting professional development is One Medical's primary value proposition for retaining human-centric team members." Christine Morehead, One Medical's Chief People Officer, adds, "As leaders, we are responsible for developing tools, resources, and programs that foster personal and professional growth that promotes team member well-being and enables One Medical to achieve its transformative, human-centered, team-based mission." At One Medical, development programs start with leadership.

## LEARNING JOURNEYS FROM THE TOP

In *When Fish Fly: Lessons for Creating a Vital and Energized Workplace from the World Famous Pike Place Fish Market*, a book I coauthored with Johnny Yokoyama, Johnny opined, "Fish smell from the head," meaning organizations are only as good as their leaders. In turn, leaders are only as good as the training and mentorship they receive.

Josh Bersin, author of *The Blended Learning Book: Best Practices, Proven Methodologies, and Lessons Learned*, conducted multiple studies on leadership development from 2005–2023. Based on his observations, Josh reports, "The level of maturity, investment, and focus on leadership has really declined." His research also suggests:

- Only 25% of companies believe their leadership development is delivering high value to the company.
- Only 24% of companies say their model is "up to date" or "highly relevant."

- Only 11% of companies embrace mentoring, and only 18% give coaching to managers and leaders.
- Only 15% of companies take care of leaders and actively monitor and mitigate leader burnout.
- Only 17% of companies are growing their leadership development budgets.

Contrary to these trends, One Medical has invested heavily in leadership development, as exemplified by the One Medical Leader Academy. One Medical describes the Leader Academy as:

*[A] progressive leadership development program designed to empower leaders at every stage of their careers and reinforce achieving the mission of transforming healthcare for all through a human-centered, technology-powered model. The Academy builds leadership capabilities to drive growth and performance and deepen leadership, clinical, and operational skills and capabilities.*

The One Medical Leader Academy consists of the "emerging leader program," "new leader orientation" (nlo), "role-specific training" (rst), "leader essentials," and "lead@OM." (*See figure below.*)

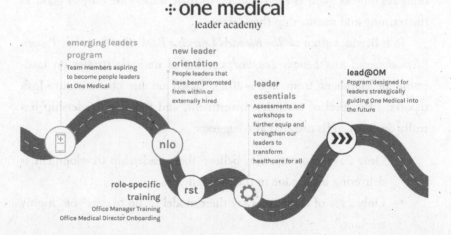

**one medical**
leader academy

**emerging leaders program**
Team members aspiring to become people leaders at One Medical

**new leader orientation**
People leaders that have been promoted from within or externally hired

**leader essentials**
Assessments and workshops to further equip and strengthen our leaders to transform healthcare for all

**lead@OM**
Program designed for leaders strategically guiding One Medical into the future

nlo

**role-specific training**
Office Manager Training
Office Medical Director Onboarding

rst

Cherie Woodbury, One Medical's Head of Talent Management, reports that leadership development programs (like all development efforts) at One Medical have evolved into learning journeys or pathways:

Once we reached a level of organizational maturity, we brought in key stakeholders to look at our development programs and knitted job skills and core competencies together into role-specific learning journeys. We explored these learning journeys for individual contributors and all levels of leadership. Through our evolution, we've created an instructional design and multimedia team to facilitate blended learning. We've also focused on pre- and post-learning touchpoints, making learning interactions more frequent. For example, instead of leadership development being event-based, we created a cadence where, within your first 90 days, you will receive a welcome to the company. Assuming you are an office manager, you would then go through office manager training and new leader orientation. Our offerings blend core competencies with the skills necessary to be successful in your role and, more broadly, as a leader at One Medical.

The office manager training mentioned by Cherie is part of One Medical's "role-specific training," which focuses on role expectations, team development, team support, patient services, leaders' standard work, and active daily management tools. By contrast, the "new leader orientation" referenced by Cherie consists of a deep dive into One Medical's vision and DNA. The new leader orientation also includes modules on "C-I-CARE for Leaders," "TOPS for Leaders," "Gemba for Leaders," and other resources. New leader orientation is held monthly. Upon completing that orientation, participants are asked to rate One Medical on the Employee Net Promoter Score (eNPS). The eNPS is calculated like the customer-facing NPS discussed in chapter 5—except employees are asked to rate the likelihood they would recommend their company to friends and colleagues. The eNPS for new leader orientation graduates is an impressive 87.

One Medical's Director of Talent Management, Eujin Ahn, suggests all One Medical manager and leadership development initiatives are "anchored to our mission, DNA, and C-I-CARE. We need leaders to embody our DNA, live C-I-CARE, and reinforce these cultural elements daily."

Specific to the "emerging leader program," which is designed to prepare team members for roles as Office Managers, Office Medical Directors, Lab Service Managers, and Virtual Medical Directors, individuals must apply for the developmental opportunity, have a strong performance rating, and garner a recommendation from their manager or a district manager. From a content perspective, the emerging leader program, launched in 2021, focuses on strengthening leadership competencies, enhancing emotional intelligence, developing team engagement skills, improving communication effectiveness, facilitating collaboration, providing constructive feedback, and bolstering leadership courage.

Eujin reports that the emerging leader program has produced valuable results for participants and One Medical:

> Over 200 people have graduated from the emerging leader program, and we are proud to have had 72 promotions into leadership from the program. In addition to advancing people into positions like office managers, we've also had a lot of success in the clinical tracks for clinicians who didn't have formal management training and want to learn how to lead colleagues and teams. An added benefit is the awareness participants gain about what it means to be a leader. For example, some people graduate from the program and decide not to become an office manager or medical director. However, they appreciate One Medical's investment in them and

stay with us. In the clinical realm, we have a retention rate of more than 95% for graduates.

One Medical has a suite of resources called "leadership essentials" that includes experiential learning about receiving and offering feedback, managing challenging conversations, and effectively navigating change. Leadership essentials also include opportunities for leaders to evaluate their personality profiles using the DiSC and to learn to use the GROW coaching model.

The DiSC is a self-assessment tool for personality traits related to dominance, influence, steadiness, and conscientiousness. It is used across industries and continents for personal development, team building, and culture enhancement.

The GROW model, first presented in John Whitmore's 1992 book, *Coaching for Performance,* is a four-step approach to goal setting and attainment. GROW is an acronym for goal, reality, obstacles/options, and way forward/will. The GROW model emphasizes the importance of asking questions instead of giving directions. The GROW questioning process facilitates SMART goals (specific, measurable, actionable/achievable, realistic/relevant, and time bound), which are realistically evaluated. Leaders help individuals or teams consider and remove obstacles while maximizing options for goal attainment. Once the path to accomplishing a goal is envisioned, leaders help their direct reports and teams develop action plans and track progress toward goal achievement.

The GROW model is an increasingly popular approach for leaders because it emphasizes coaching over compliance. In a *Harvard Business Review* article titled "The Leader as Coach," Herminia Ibarra and Anne Scoular note:

> The role of the manager, in short, is becoming that of a coach. This is a dramatic and fundamental shift, and we've observed it first-hand. Over the past decade, we've seen it in our ongoing research on how organizations are transforming themselves for the digital age . . . Increasingly, coaching is becoming integral to the fabric of a learning culture—a skill that good managers at all levels need to

develop and deploy . . . It's work that all managers should engage in with all their people all the time, in ways that help define the organization's culture and advance its mission.[6]

In addition to leadership development tools for emerging leaders and established leaders, One Medical offers an executive leadership program called Lead at One Medical or Lead@OM.

According to Eujin Ahn, Director of Talent Management,

Lead@OM is a comprehensive program that includes 360 assessments through which leaders receive feedback from multiple raters. The goal is to garner a comprehensive view of the executive's strengths and improvement opportunities, build on their strengths, and mitigate deficits. We also leverage the model championed by Kouzes and Posner in their book *Leadership Challenge*, which involves inspiring a shared vision, challenging the process, encouraging the heart, and enabling others to act.

Due to One Medical's focus on managerial and leadership development, Eujin describes the company's evolution and readiness for exponential growth:

When I came to One Medical in 2021, senior leaders communicated a need to build managerial and leadership bench strength. Thanks to the "emerging leader program" and the rest of our leadership development resources, we have a talent pipeline primed to grow at the speed of Amazon.

## FROM LEADERSHIP SKILLS TO INDIVIDUAL CONTRIBUTOR DEVELOPMENT

In addition to manager and leadership training, One Medical drives skills and competencies for individual contributors through One Medical University (OMU). OMU is a learning hub that combines self-guided and facilitated sessions across varied roles. Topics covered in OMU include career development, projecting confidence, and business basics. The courses are designed to accommodate diverse schedules. Additionally, every team member receives a LinkedIn Learning license to facilitate self-guided learning.

Donna Mosich, Senior Manager of Learning & Development, shares how One Medical enhances training for individual contributors in non-clinical roles:

> For example, we have developed a scalable, independent learning experience coupled with focused instructor-led training for our Member Support Specialists (MSS). The goals of this enhanced learning approach are to ensure MSS Front Desk team members are quickly grounded in our core principles and learn what is needed to deliver outstanding patient and care team experiences. This holistic training incorporates eLearnings housed on our Continu LMS platform, knowledge checks, practice worksheets, a buddy system that supports on-the-job application, and a final test to assess mastery. It also provides tools for managers and leaders to participate in and reinforce the MSS's skill development. The program also benefits from being supported by learning development specialists on the talent management team who integrate core elements to maximize learning effectiveness for adult learners. This program exemplifies our overall approach to helping our team members engage, learn, and grow at One Medical.

(*See figure on the following page for an overview of the first 30 days of the MSS Training and Onboarding program.*)

From the perspective of skill development for clinicians, One Medical leaders focus on:

**Clinician continuing education programs that support engagement, ongoing development, and retention. These programs are designed to equip clinicians with the knowledge, skills, and behaviors to improve their clinical practice while driving business performance and outcomes.**

# New Approach

| Days 1–2 | Days 3–8 | Days 6–30 |
|---|---|---|
| **New hire orientation** | **Role-specific training** | **Reinforce training** |
| Day 1: Employees receive orientation to: | Complete Units 1 to 6 of eLearning, knowledge checks, and worksheets | Identify what new hires are expected to do and reinforce it by reviewing Units in Continu |
|    Mission | | |
|    Culture | | |
|    Business | 2-hour sessions with MSS trainers for teachbacks | Reinforcement, practice, and test out |
|    CICARE | | |
| Day 2: Tech resources/office orientation w/ instructor, set up technology and intro to basic system | Align with office buddies for shadowing, reviewing checklists, and tracking progress | Build out metrics that capture what is successful or not working |

**Who qualifies as a buddy?**
*A person that has mastery in the role, is interested in training, and wants to share their skills. It could be a shift lead, MSS level II, or person from a different office that wants a stretch assignment.*

Leadership's strategic goal for continuing education for clinicians is to position One Medical "as the destination for Primary Care Provider learning and professional development across the career journey." To that end, leaders have developed a multiyear training framework for performance pillars and outcomes related to clinical quality, health equity, and practice sustainability.

Spencer Blackman, MD, Senior Director of Clinical Education, who has helped develop clinical training at One Medical since 2010, highlights One Medical's foundational commitment to clinical training:

> In the early days of One Medical, a commonly held perception among clinicians coming out of formal education was that if you wanted to practice good medicine, you worked in a university hospital–based setting. If you worked in community settings like ours, you would inevitably fall behind cutting-edge best practices. Since we were aspirational and had a commitment to academics, the clinical staff divided up responsibility for scanning, reviewing, and summarizing 20 top medical journals. Over time, that has evolved into a role for several clinicians who are medical writers, and they incorporate trends beyond academic research. We call the

summary Big Medical News. This not only helps keep clinicians current but it saves them time.

From the inception of One Medical, Tom Lee and his small group of clinical colleagues started their Wednesdays an hour early—so they could reserve the last hour to do "rounds." During those rounds, they would either work on improving One Medical, review a clinical item, or invite specialists to teach them something new. In the process, they strengthened relationships with those specialists. This approach is similar to learning delivered during Grand Rounds in a hospital setting. Over the years, we refined the process and called it "National Rounds." We still meet weekly and present broadly applicable content for all our clinicians.

In addition to National Rounds, Spencer adds:

While workgroup-specific rounds are always evolving as One Medical grows and changes, we currently produce rounds for pediatricians, expanded-hours providers, virtual providers, office-based providers, and RNs. To further ensure we stay current in the broad and constantly changing field of primary care, we have groups of subject matter experts assembled in domain working groups and Medical Advisory Councils. These groups of providers have expertise in areas like mental or cardiovascular health, field requests from One Medical providers, and offer clinical guidance. For example, a clinician might submit a question to the cardiovascular working group that asks, "Should we be using a recently released risk calculator? If so, how should we use it?" The working group will review that calculator, look at the supporting research, possibly reach out to a cardiologist we work with, discuss the topic, and tender recommendations. If the recommendations are broad, we call them a guideline. If the recommendations are narrow, we call them a practice bulletin. Our intranet has a growing body of internal guidelines, practice bulletins, and external resources on primary care standards.

Our communication platform has a list of clinical channels where providers learn from each other and interact thousands of times a day. I sit in the cardiology channel and comment on EKGs, cholesterol levels, and palpitation discussions throughout the day.

One Medical Regional Director and Vice President of Provider Engagement, Ron Englert, adds:

The developmental resources at One Medical are outstanding, and clinicians highly value the community-building benefits of processes like National and workgroup-specific rounds. Primary care can be demanding, and clinicians draw strength and connection from being with one another. I've seen an increase in provider engagement as we seek to do more rounding and offer other provider experiences in person rather than via video conference.

Clinicians who serve Medicare populations also receive training specific to value-based care and clinical geriatrics. These training resources equip clinicians to practice in a geriatric-focused, risk-based model. The eNPS for participants in this program is an extraordinary 94.

One Medical's Head of Talent Management, Cherie Woodbury, explains how her team approaches training for clinical and non-clinical individual contributors:

Our approach to organization-wide talent development is systematic as opposed to programmatic. Our systems include a talent management hub, a human resource hub, fully blended learning, and consulting services from my team. We have a learning management system, train-the-trainer components, and an evolving mentorship program. We leverage the best of technology and blend it with human-centered learning. My team also does organizational development and consulting—including instructional design, compliance, operations, clinical education, leadership, and job skills. We also have a federated model where we are a centralized resource that helps leaders with performance management, talent reviews, and succession planning.

Eujin Ahn expands on One Medical's blended learning approach, noting, "We combine asynchronous e-learning with pre-work and immersive, experiential instructor-led training. This hybrid approach results in better experiences, an improved learning cadence, and greater activation of information."

**QUICK CHECKUP**

To what degree do you provide a blended learning approach that includes asynchronous e-learning with pre-work and immersive, experiential instructor-led training?

One Medical's commitment to career development is valued by team members, fosters employee retention, and attracts new hires. Natasha Bhuyan, MD, a Scottsdale-based clinician, explains:

I tell family, friends, and colleagues that joining One Medical is the best career decision I could have ever made. I was attracted to the company's continuous improvement culture and leadership's commitment to professional development. One Medical invests in training and provides opportunities to take on diverse roles, and the ROI on those investments is engagement and retention.

Diana Vinh, a Senior Office Manager overseeing multiple Arizona clinics, emphasizes the value of leadership developmental opportunities like the Emerging Leader Program.

I originally applied to One Medical for an office manager position after spending 15 years as a retail store manager. I didn't get the office manager position but was selected as a shift lead. That meant I served at the front desk part-time and did inventory the remainder of the time. Not long into my employment at One Medical, I was chosen to participate in the first cohort of the Emerging Leader Program.

Despite all those years as a retail manager, the Emerging Leaders Program opened my eyes to what it meant to lead people, provide feedback, and demonstrate courage. I also learned the importance of acknowledging when I don't have an answer and networking with peers to get the necessary information. I am close with my peers from the program, and we reach out to one another regularly. Based on the value I gained from the Emerging Leader Program, I've become a program facilitator related to emotional intelligence.

Before we explore how One Medical's team member development contributes to program development, let's take a moment to apply human growth and development lessons from One Medical to ensure you are Winning Through People & Technology.

WINNING
THROUGH PEOPLE
& TECHNOLOGY

1. How does your company or department compare with research suggesting that 70% of employees feel they lack the skills needed to do their jobs? More specifically, what skills must be mastered based on current and future business needs? What deficits, if any, does your organization or department have related to these skills?

2. Does your organization have a progressive leadership development program designed to empower leaders at every stage of their careers and reinforce achieving your organizational mission? If so, describe your program. If not, identify gaps and what it would take to address them.

3. How does your organization or department identify and develop emerging leaders? How effective are your efforts in helping high-performing individuals advance to leadership or decide they are better suited to stay in individual contributor roles? What data do you have to verify the success of your initiatives?

4. How do you help leaders evaluate their personality profiles (e.g., DiSC) to increase self-awareness, team building, and culture? How effective are these efforts? If you aren't providing personality profile tools to leaders, why not, and what benefits may you gain if you did?

5. Do you accept Herminia Ibarra and Anne Scoular's premise that the manager's role is becoming that of a coach? If not, why not? If so, how are you fostering coach skills for your managers and leaders?

6. How do your leadership development programs compare with the One Medical Leader Academy? Similarly, how do your individual contributor training programs compare to One Medical University?

## EXPANDING PRODUCTS AND SERVICES

While attracting and developing talent is mission critical for a rapidly growing company, expanding services, developing new and relevant programs, and increasing brand awareness are equally crucial. Let's take a look at some of One Medical's service expansions.

Former One Medical CEO Amir Dan Rubin credits a notable portion of the company's growth to providing a natural extension of primary care services to family medicine and pediatrics, which resulted in employers extending One Medical membership to dependents. Amir notes:

We realized that since we serve employers, we must also serve their dependents. So, we grew family medicine and pediatric services. As a result, we saw a sizable increase in companies offering One Medical as a dependent benefit—from 71% to 85%. By the time I left One Medical, almost all business clients were extending membership benefits to dependents.

By designing offices geared to family medicine and pediatrics (*see figure below*), One Medical's leaders positioned the company to:

> [T]reat people of all ages, every member of your family—from newborns to great-grandparents . . . When a provider treats multiple members of a family, they can gain unique insight into their lives, health histories, and wellness goals . . . Family medicine providers are trained to provide preventive care as well as care for urgent and chronic issues for adults and pediatric patients alike. This includes the diagnosis and treatment of everyday illnesses and infections (like colds, flu, and ear infections) as well as chronic conditions such as asthma, diabetes, ADD and ADHD, arthritis, and heart disease.[7]

### Employers: Dependents

**Making life better for employees and their dependents**

 Office-based pediatrics and family medicine

 24/7 virtual care for the family

 Lactation consulting

Will Kimbrough, MD, evaluates potential areas of growth and expansion based on their relevance to primary care, potential to address patient needs, and impact on healthcare partners. Will explains:

> I start by asking if the service or program fits into primary care. It's easy to get distracted by ideas outside of primary care when ample opportunities to craft exciting projects in our area exist. If the service fits with primary care, we need to determine what problem

the program addresses and the likely benefits relative to the investment. We must also consider the service's feasibility and impact on our healthcare partners. For example, if we expand into an area, will it make life better or worse for our patients and partners?

Using these filters, Will offers an example of Zio patch monitoring, a service expansion One Medical rolled out in 2023.

A Zio patch is an ambulatory EKG monitor that a patient will wear for typically two weeks to detect arrhythmias. EKG monitoring has historically been in the realm of cardiology. However, clinical studies on the accuracy and performance of the Zio patch have shown that it can be safely brought into primary care. Before using it at One Medical, we talked to our health system partners. We determined that their cardiology departments were overwhelmed with patients needing more specialized services, and they were happy to have us take on this type of monitoring. As a result, in some of our regions, wait times for a referral to a cardiologist went from almost two months to getting someone in the same day. Now, instead of a cardiologist reading normal test reports, we can interpret those reports safely and triage high-acuity patients to those specialists so those patients can be seen quickly.

Similarly, One Medical is tracking and considering new technologies, like an FDA-cleared AI-powered device that examines moles to determine if they are likely melanoma. Since skin screenings fit into primary care and take up considerable time for dermatologists, One Medical will evaluate the viability of using this type of tool to screen and refer patients based on their high risk for melanoma or other acute dermatologic needs.

Will adds that there is an abundance of ideas and service expansion projects always being considered by One Medical leaders.

We keep a list of ideas that our teams identify as patient needs. One item that was added to the list recently involved vasectomies. That procedure often has multi-month waiting lists in some of our regions. Given the priorities of urologists, there are usually only a few clinic days per month for vasectomies. One Medical may never be in the business of providing vasectomies, but every few months, we evaluate ideas like this one through the lens of "Is this primary care?" and "Will it fill a gap and delight our members?"

Behavioral health services undeniably met Will's program expansion criteria. In chapter 3, I cited research from the National Survey on Drug Use and Health, the Anxiety and Depression Association of America, and the National Alliance on Mental Illness concerning the United States' substance abuse and mental health crisis. In that chapter, I also highlighted, in the context of employer benefits, One Medical's integrated care model for behavioral health.

One Medical started providing behavioral health services as part of contracts with employers. For some larger companies, One Medical provided co-located care (placing therapists at the company's on-site primary care clinic). Other companies contracted for a set number of sessions per employee or paid for the mental health services used by their employees. Over time, One Medical has looked for ways to expand integrated behavioral healthcare to all members.

Will Kimbrough explains:

We learned a lot about delivering behavioral health services through our offerings to enterprise clients and knew we would move towards a broader program. The pandemic also taught us that virtual mental health care produced similar outcomes to in-person treatment, lower no-show rates, and comparable patient satisfaction. Our clinical care team also loved the ability to refer patients to One Medical behavioral health services without struggling to find a provider in their market or having the member use a search engine to locate a therapist. While we were working on scaling behavior health in 2019, we leaned heavily into virtual therapy and hired Andrew Bertagnolli to help us develop a comprehensive approach.

Andrew Bertagnolli, PhD, One Medical's National Director of Virtual Behavioral Health Services, is a licensed clinical psychologist who has worked as the Director of Integrated Behavioral Health at Kaiser Permanente and the Vice President of Clinical Product Care/Case Management and Recovery Programs for Optum. Since joining One Medical in 2020, Andrew and his team have developed a primary care–based behavioral health service for pediatric, student, adult, and senior populations. Andrew explains the evolution of the program, noting:

> Early on, we had to understand and have confidence in our collaborative care service and its billing mechanism. We also had to hire and increase One Medical's behavioral health team and ensure members of that team had relevant licenses to practice across the United States. Over time, we have built an effective model where the primary care provider oversees the patient's care in partnership with our behavioral health team. Whenever a member has a behavioral need, the primary care provider can make a referral to our "Mindset" program. We then conduct an intake, and our care managers, therapists, and psychiatrists provide the services needed, such as medication consultation, care navigation, coaching, skills activation, and regular contact.

In addition to referrals that come directly from primary care providers, Andrew's team also responds to mental health crisis calls and elevated responses to mental health screening questionnaires. For example:

> Our member-facing app automatically and routinely prompts members to complete behavioral health questionnaires. When a patient's responses hit certain thresholds for issues like an elevated suicide risk, it pops into my team's work task queue, and it is immediately routed to a team member licensed in the

state where the member lives. That team member follows the well-researched "caring contacts" model by reaching out to the member, expressing the appropriate level of concern, and communicating our desire to book a one-time meeting to discuss their needs and do a further risk assessment. Depending on their situation, we will likely refer them for an intake in our "Mindset" program or provide crisis resources for "in the moment" support. We have slightly different workflows depending on the severity of their symptoms and if they have an upcoming appointment with their primary care provider (PCP). Just as the member's screening questionnaire results alert their PCP via the electronic health record (EHR), we also communicate with the PCP directly and through the EHR.

One Medical's Will Kimbrough, MD, who is also a board-certified internist, shares how One Medical's evolving integrated behavioral health offerings benefit patients:

A couple of months ago, I received an alert through our EHR that a patient I hadn't seen in a while reported moderate depression symptoms on a mental health screen pushed to him through the app. I sent him a note saying, "How are you doing? Should we touch base?" He scheduled an appointment for the next day, and we talked about how he had spent hundreds of dollars out of pocket for a private psychiatrist who prescribed a brand-name medication that caused substantial side effects. The patient also reported that he couldn't find a therapist covered by his insurance. So, through my lens as his primary care physician, I was glad to look for other generic medication options and refer him to Andrew's "Mindset" program so he could access in-network therapy options, a care manager who will stay in close contact with him, community resource referrals, and assistance from a psychiatrist if we need to make medication adjustments. We are also using regular surveys to track his depression symptoms.

Let's shift gears from program growth to brand awareness and member growth strategies, but before we do, let's take a moment to apply product and program extension lessons from One Medical to ensure you are Winning Through People & Technology.

## WINNING THROUGH PEOPLE & TECHNOLOGY

1. How are you expanding your services to broader audiences?
2. What adjacent locations represent natural extensions of your core offerings?
3. How does your department or organization decide which projects or programs you will consider developing? What filters do you use? (For instance, does it fit our core competencies? What is the program's likely impact relative to cost? How feasible is the program? Is there a viable reimbursement model? How will the introduction of this program affect all of our stakeholders?)
4. Do you keep a list of ideas that could address areas of customer need? If so, what process do you use to routinely consider program development opportunities from that list? If you don't have a list, start by considering three specific customer needs and what your department or organization can do to address them.
5. How might you apply lessons from One Medical's expansion of behavioral health services (e.g., garner learning from one area of your business to apply to broader applications, do comparative analyses of service delivery such as the efficacy of in-person vs. virtual care)?

## EXPANDING BRAND AWARENESS

Brand awareness has been challenging for One Medical since the company was founded. Imagine having a limited marketing budget and trying to get enough attention from consumers and business leaders to explain a somewhat complex value proposition. That explanation would need to succinctly outline a revolutionary membership-based primary care model being delivered in clinics primarily concentrated around San Francisco. While One Medical grew from word-of-mouth referrals and a talented business-to-business sales team, Doug Sweeny was recruited in 2018 to join then CEO Amir Dan Rubin and the senior leadership team at One Medical to lead brand strategy, product marketing, creative, advertising, social media, public relationship, partner marketing, and e-commerce.

Doug is a veteran executive who previously led marketing for global brands such as Adidas, Levi's, General Motors EV1, and Nest. *Forbes* also named him among the top 50 Chief Marketing Officers in 2018. Having been a member of One Medical before joining the leadership team, Doug felt his initial value would be to ensure marketing assets and One Medical's brand positioning matched the extraordinary member experience. He also perceived a need:

> [T]o accelerate the revenue and business flywheel. One Medical was growing but not at an exponential rate. Amir was embarking on raising money to build more clinics, forge healthcare partnerships, and strengthen our technology infrastructure. From a marketing perspective, we focused on driving revenue by communicating our mission and helping people understand what made us vastly different from other primary care companies. That difference was our "real-life care." Even with low consumer expectations, other healthcare providers often disappointed patients. By contrast, if a One Medical member was sick at 2 in the morning, they could engage in a video visit at no cost and no copay. They could even get their prescription delivered to their door if they went through other services. We knew One Medical should be their choice if they wanted frictionless "real-life" care.

Doug also saw an opportunity to transition One Medical's branding elements from a "start-up feel" to something more premium, modern, and emotionally resonant. According to Doug, his team, aided by outside consultants:

[R]edesigned the logo and created a tool kit for the brand's look and feel. We married modernity with One Medical's human emotional components to ensure our imagery was elevated but accessible to the consumer. We sought to create a design system matching best-in-class brands like Nike and Airbnb. We needed something appropriate for the visual age consistent with our product and service offerings. We also had to ensure maximal returns from our design and marketing efforts.

One Medical's design system focused on respecting people, simplifying the complex, making premium care accessible, and treating humans, not illnesses.

To spend marketing dollars wisely, Doug and his team examined how people choose physicians. Unlike his experiences driving transactions for a long-standing brand like Levi's, healthcare consumers made relational healthcare decisions based on recommendations and a brand's presence in a community. When One Medical entered a new market, Doug notes:

We ran full-funnel campaigns. In a city like San Diego, we would advertise on everything from TV to rail lines in and out of the city. Everything we did was localized. If we enlisted aerial advertising with planes flying over beaches, we would target messages about getting care when you get sick during your vacation. We had a national playbook that we tailored for relevance in local communities.

The images on page 178 show examples of localized marketing in New York's Times Square and in San Diego.

One Medical's refreshing approach to brand marketing has garnered substantial praise from marketing experts. For example, a 2023 Branding Elm case study noted:

One Medical has a unique branding strategy that has been able to stand out in a crowded market . . . The company's branding is built around a clean, modern aesthetic that is designed to appeal to a younger, tech-savvy demographic . . . One Medical's branding strategy has paid off in a big way. The company has seen impressive growth in recent years . . . One Medical's patient retention rate is significantly higher than the industry average, with many patients citing the company's branding and approach as the reason for their loyalty . . . One of the most significant impacts of One Medical's branding strategy has been on the perception of medical brands in general. Before One Medical, medical brands were often viewed as cold, impersonal, and bureaucratic . . . Today, medical brands are increasingly focused on creating a positive patient experience, and many are adopting similar branding strategies to One Medical's.[8]

In 2022, Chris Hollander followed Doug Sweeny as One Medical's Chief Marketing Officer. Chris also brought vast marketing experience to One Medical from prior roles as Director of Marketing for TM Pepsi, Chief Marketing Officer at Panera, and Chief Growth Officer at Iora Health.

Despite the transformational impact of One Medical's brand and marketing strategies, the company has struggled to garner brand awareness. Chris Hollander reports: "As great as One Medical is, we only had 15% aided awareness nationally. For us to realize our mission's full transformational impact, we needed more people to know about and choose us."

Leaders at One Medical take a strategic approach to drive awareness, website traffic, and conversions by first understanding segments of primary care consumers and how One Medical's value proposition aligns with each group. For ease of explanation, I will categorize four primary care segments using labels I created based on their value drivers. Each group, which I will describe in brief, represents roughly 25% of the overall population of primary care patients:

- **Experience**—This group tends to be older than the average primary care patient, has a somewhat higher income, and is more likely to have a college degree. This experience-focused group seeks a balance of technology and human-delivered care and represents about 50% of One Medical's members.

- **Technology**—This segment is "all in" on technology. They are primarily attracted to digital tools that enable scheduling, provider communication, and access to their health information. This group represents about 35% of One Medical members.
- **Efficiency**—This primary care consumer group seeks ease of access and efficiency. They are less interested in care relationships or longer appointments and want to be seen as swiftly as possible when they perceive the need for care.
- **Status Quo**—This group is comfortable with how primary care has been practiced and places less value on innovation or interactive technology.

One Medical's former Chief Marketing Officer, Chris Hollander, explains the strategic relevance of understanding consumer segments when it comes to brand awareness and attracting prospects:

Segmentation research helps us better target our audiences. It assists us in understanding people who value what we offer and are likely to choose and stay with One Medical. We are not suitable for everyone. People must be willing to pay a membership, feel comfortable using an app, and want efficient but unhurried relationships with providers. We over-index in some segments, as 85% of our members come from 50% of the primary care population, and that shows us that we have opportunities to communicate our value proposition to more individuals who are likely to appreciate what we provide.

QUICK
CHECKUP

How effectively do you use segmentation research to understand and
target your key consumer segments?

Thanks to Amazon, One Medical has many more resources available to
garner consumers' attention. Chris shares:

> We now have a broader team thinking about One Medical's mar-
> keting than we did before we joined Amazon. We also have exciting
> ways to drive traffic. For example, before Amazon, we could buy
> paid social ads and drive people to the One Medical site—if we
> needed a traffic generator. Contrast that to the traffic we received
> when Amazon's CEO Andy Jassy posted his letter announcing our
> partnership on Amazon's home page or the traffic we now garner
> from being on the health tab at Amazon.com. Also, when Ama-
> zon made One Medical an add-on option for Prime members in
> November of 2023, we had membership-oriented people becoming
> aware of One Medical and visiting our site. I also benefit from
> working with amazingly talented marketing partners on the Ama-
> zon side who are helping us unlock opportunities to drive aware-
> ness, traffic, and conversions.

Chris's comments are a perfect segue into chapter 7, which will examine how One Medical and Amazon are aligning to drive One Medical's
sustained growth. However, before we get to that alignment, let's take a
moment to look at this chapter's Transformational Lessons.

# TRANSFORMATIONAL LESSONS

- MIT professor Peter Senge describes learning organizations as continually expanding their capacity to create their future.
- Labor costs account for up to 70% of a company's operating expenses.
- According to McKinsey's research, high performers are 800% more productive in highly complex occupations.
- Seventy percent of employees report that they don't have mastery of the skills needed to do their job, and 47% are dissatisfied with their employer's learning and development program.
- Eighty percent of CEOs say skill shortages threaten their companies' growth and are stunting innovation, hurting quality, and limiting the pursuit of market opportunities.
- According to One Medical's founder, Tom Lee, MD, "Developing people builds a stronger culture, fuels growth, and drives sustainability."
- The One Medical Leadership Academy is a progressive leadership development program designed to empower leaders at every stage of their careers. It reinforces achieving the mission of transforming healthcare for all through a human-centered, technology-powered model.
- Among other metrics, One Medical evaluates employee engagement related to training and development using the Employee Net Promoter Score (eNPS). The eNPS is calculated similarly to the customer-facing NPS but asks team members about their likelihood of recommending their company to friends and colleagues.
- The DiSC is a self-assessment tool for personality traits related to dominance, influence, steadiness, and conscientiousness.

- The GROW coaching model stands for goal, reality, obstacles/options, and way forward/will. It emphasizes the importance of asking questions instead of giving directions. This questioning process facilitates SMART goals (specific, measurable, actionable/achievable, realistic/relevant, and time bound), which are realistically evaluated.
- One Medical University (OMU) is a learning hub that combines self-guided and facilitated sessions across varied roles. Topics covered in OMU include career development, projecting confidence, and business basics.
- Leaders at One Medical evaluate potential areas of growth and expansion based on their relevance to primary care, potential to address patient needs, and impact on healthcare partners.
- One Medical maintains a list of ideas team members identify as patient needs. Growth ideas on those lists are evaluated every few months.
- Segmentation research helps marketers target audiences. It increases their understanding of the people who value a brand's offerings and identifies those likely to choose and stay with the brand.

## CHAPTER 7

# Growing Together

> The most important single thing is to focus
> obsessively on the customer. Our goal is to be
> Earth's most customer-centric company . . .
> The keys to success are patience, persistence,
> and obsessive attention to detail.
>
> **Jeff Bezos, founder, Amazon**[1]

Until now, I have focused on human-centered, technology-powered elements of One Medical that made the company attractive to Amazon and how those elements can be applied to foster growth and impact for your business. Now, let's look at One Medical's journey since being acquired by Amazon in July 2022. Additionally, let's examine the challenges and opportunities Amazon One Medical (the new brand name that rolled out starting in June 2024) faces in the years ahead.

Throughout my career, I've been fortunate to consult for and write about brands that attracted acquisition. For example, I wrote *The New Gold*

*Standard: 5 Leadership Principles for Creating a Legendary Customer Experience Courtesy of the Ritz-Carlton Hotel Company* in 2008, after Marriott International Incorporated acquired The Ritz-Carlton Hotel Company. Also, after Amazon acquired the shoe and clothing retailer Zappos in 2011, I released *The Zappos Experience: 5 Principles to Inspire, Engage, and WOW.* By working with those companies in their post-acquisition phase, I appreciate the promise and pain of synthesizing business cultures.

On the promise side, Neil Lindsay, Senior Vice President of Amazon Health Services (AHS), explains the unique attraction to One Medical:

> I'd been a member for a few years before we acquired them, and the One Medical experience always felt fundamentally different and better than anything I experienced in primary care. That difference is the result of customer obsession—one of Amazon's core principles. My experiences as a One Medical member, along with interactions I had with then-CEO Amir Rubin, highlighted other similarities between the Amazon and One Medical cultures. Historically, at Amazon, our bias has been to build, not buy. When we acquire a company, we are looking for businesses that deliver outstanding experiences that we can help elevate, scale, and expand. Those rare companies must have skill sets and capabilities that we don't necessarily possess. They must also be inventive.
>
> We believe and often say it's "always day one." There's always something new to invent. Given the divine discontent of customers—where yesterday's invention is today's new normal— we embrace discontent and get up every single day to invent on our customers' behalf to make their lives easier and better. We seized the opportunity to acquire One Medical to leverage our commonalities (customer obsession, culture, invention) and scale their complementary human-centered and technology-powered strengths.

Like all mergers and acquisitions, Amazon has and will continue to have challenges as it seeks to realize One Medical's full potential. Kison

Patel, CEO and founder of DealRoom, emphasizes that many hurdles will be encountered throughout the post-acquisition phase:

> While M&A practitioners have adopted the widespread stance that integration is absolutely necessary for the long-term success of a merger or acquisition, the process is nonetheless fraught with difficulties. Signing the dotted line on a transaction is, in many cases, the easy part. Extracting value from integration is a far more complex question.

Kison outlines widespread integration issues that must be addressed consistently throughout the post-acquisition phase. They include sustaining momentum for the acquired and acquiring business, maintaining employee and customer engagement, navigating senior leadership changes, addressing potential culture shifts, integrating technology systems, having the courage to make big decisions that drive expected efficiencies and capitalize on strengths, and communicating effectively within and across the newly merged organizations.

Since acquiring One Medical, Amazon leaders have already faced many of these challenges. For example, on the leadership front, One Medical's CEO, Amir Dan Rubin, left the company a year after the acquisition to launch and lead his venture capital firm focused on healthcare innovation—Healthier Capital. Similarly, Stuart Parmenter, One Medical's Chief Technology Officer, who led technology strategy for eight years, left the company to pursue other opportunities.

---

**QUICK CHECKUP**

How effectively has your organization navigated leadership transitions? How will your succession plan ensure business continuity when key leaders depart?

Concerning the courage needed to make big decisions, Amazon initiated a round of layoffs in February 2024 at One Medical and Amazon Pharmacy (the evolution of Amazon's PillPack acquisition in 2018). In a memo to employees announcing the layoffs, Neil Lindsay, Senior Vice President of Amazon Health Services, noted:

> As we continue to make it easier for people to get and stay healthy, we have identified areas where we can reposition resources so we can invest in invention and experiences that have a direct impact on our customers and members of all ages. Unfortunately, these changes will result in the elimination of a few hundred roles across One Medical and Amazon Pharmacy.[2]

One Medical CEO Trent Green suggests the 2024 staff reductions were made as a continuation of the integration of One Medical's prior acquisition of Iora Health:

> One Medical is continuously improving and evaluating ways to streamline operations. This is especially important given how Amazon can drive member acquisition as part of an opportunity to add a One Medical membership via Prime. In my experience, healthcare organizations tend to throw people at problems. For example, if you wanted to engage more members, you might hire 15 people to get on the phone and drive that engagement. Now, technology allows us to automate our outreach.
>
> Additionally, we hadn't fully integrated Iora Health, the senior health company we acquired in September 2021. So, these staffing changes resulted from harmonizing our member support model by leveraging our central administrative contact center and extending our virtual medical teams to support our senior health members and providers in addition to the legacy One Medical members and in-office providers. To do so, we reallocated resources from the senior health offices to centralized teams and we gained some staffing efficiency in the process.

Regarding culture, both Amazon and One Medical are human-centric and technology-powered, with a slightly different emphasis. In a conversation with Neil Lindsay, he suggests, "One Medical has emphasized human-centeredness and supported it with technology. At Amazon, we have been technology-centric with an obsession for customers."

Leaders at both companies are proud of their rich cultural foundation. One Medical's culture is founded on the company's mission, DNA, and C-I-CARE (which you have read about in chapters 2 and 5). Similarly, Amazon pursues a mission ("to be Earth's most customer-centric company, Earth's best employer, and Earth's safest place to work") by adhering to four overarching principles:

- Customer obsession rather than competitor focus
- Passion for invention
- Commitment to operational excellence
- Long-term thinking

**QUICK CHECKUP**

To what degree does your organization demonstrate:

- Customer obsession rather than competitor focus
- Passion for invention
- Commitment to operational excellence
- Long-term thinking

Amazon leaders also hold one another accountable to steward Amazon by acting in accord with 16 leadership principles:[3]

### Customer Obsession
Leaders start with the customer and work backwards. They work vigorously to earn and keep customer trust. Although leaders pay attention to competitors, they obsess over customers.

## Ownership

Leaders are owners. They think long term and don't sacrifice long-term value for short-term results. They act on behalf of the entire company, beyond just their own team. They never say "that's not my job."

## Invent and Simplify

Leaders expect and require innovation and invention from their teams and always find ways to simplify. They are externally aware, look for new ideas from everywhere, and are not limited by "not invented here." As we do new things, we accept that we may be misunderstood for long periods of time.

## Are Right, A Lot

Leaders are right a lot. They have strong judgment and good instincts. They seek diverse perspectives and work to disconfirm their beliefs.

## Learn and Be Curious

Leaders are never done learning and always seek to improve themselves. They are curious about new possibilities and act to explore them.

## Hire and Develop the Best

Leaders raise the performance bar with every hire and promotion. They recognize exceptional talent, and willingly move them throughout the organization. Leaders develop leaders and take seriously their role in coaching others. We work on behalf of our people to invent mechanisms for development like Career Choice.

## Insist on the Highest Standards

Leaders have relentlessly high standards—many people may think these standards are unreasonably high. Leaders are continually raising the bar and drive their teams to deliver high quality products, services, and processes. Leaders ensure that defects do not get sent down the line and that problems are fixed so they stay fixed.

## Think Big

Thinking small is a self-fulfilling prophecy. Leaders create and communicate a bold direction that inspires results. They think differently and look around corners for ways to serve customers.

**Bias for Action**

Speed matters in business. Many decisions and actions are reversible and do not need extensive study. We value calculated risk taking.

**Frugality**

Accomplish more with less. Constraints breed resourcefulness, self-sufficiency, and invention. There are no extra points for growing headcount, budget size, or fixed expense.

**Earn Trust**

Leaders listen attentively, speak candidly, and treat others respectfully. They are vocally self-critical, even when doing so is awkward or embarrassing. Leaders do not believe their or their team's body odor smells of perfume. They benchmark themselves and their teams against the best.

**Dive Deep**

Leaders operate at all levels, stay connected to the details, audit frequently, and are skeptical when metrics and anecdote differ. No task is beneath them.

**Have Backbone; Disagree and Commit**

Leaders are obligated to respectfully challenge decisions when they disagree, even when doing so is uncomfortable or exhausting. Leaders have conviction and are tenacious. They do not compromise for the sake of social cohesion. Once a decision is determined, they commit wholly.

**Deliver Results**

Leaders focus on the key inputs for their business and deliver them with the right quality and in a timely fashion. Despite setbacks, they rise to the occasion and never settle.

**Strive to be Earth's Best Employer**

Leaders work every day to create a safer, more productive, higher performing, more diverse, and more just work environment. They lead with empathy, have fun at work, and make it easy for others to have fun. Leaders ask themselves: Are my fellow employees growing? Are they empowered? Are they ready for what's next? Leaders have a vision for and commitment to their employees' personal success, whether that be at Amazon or elsewhere.

## Success and Scale Bring Broad Responsibility

We started in a garage, but we're not there anymore. We are big, we impact the world, and we are far from perfect. We must be humble and thoughtful about even the secondary effects of our actions. Our local communities, planet, and future generations need us to be better every day. We must begin each day with a determination to make better, do better, and be better for our customers, our employees, our partners, and the world at large. And we must end every day knowing we can do even more tomorrow. Leaders create more than they consume and always leave things better than how they found them.

So, how do you bring together two companies with similar but sufficiently different cultural infrastructures? Christine Morehead, One Medical's Chief People Officer, shares part of that process:

> We worked with an outside consultant who conducted almost 40 interviews with Amazon Pharmacy, Amazon Clinic, and One Medical leaders. We learned from these interviews that while all leaders were excited about the possibilities of working together, there were some differences in our cultures and how we approached work that we would need to align on. We brought leaders together to address this head-on and determine how to move through the storming and norming stages of development to expedite the performing stage and maximize productivity. The materials we used throughout the meeting were designed to blend our cultural languages and focus on the best elements of each culture.

Christine's references to the stages of team development come from Bruce Tuckman's FSNP model, where *F* stands for forming (putting together the team structure), *S* for storming (organizing tasks, navigating interpersonal conflicts, and addressing structural issues related to leadership and power), *N* for norming (developing group cohesion and ways to share leadership), and *P* for performing (adapting to be highly productive).

Trent Green, One Medical's CEO, provides additional insight into how Amazon and One Medical are integrating and aligning to drive productivity and performance, noting:

> I am in regular meetings with Amazon leaders, engaging in lively discussions about how to grow together to deliver an exceptional customer/member/patient experience at scale. Unlike other companies that Amazon has acquired, our integration is unique because we may be the first Amazon business where human interaction is the product—that is, a connection between a member/patient and a provider. In many other Amazon businesses, people are integral to the supply chain but not in ways comparable to the provider/patient relationship. We are in the very early innings and are learning from each other. We are benefiting greatly from Amazon's resources, customer obsession, technologies, and vision for the future of Amazon Health Services.

In support of those shared learnings, Trent adds:

> As we joined the Amazon ecosystem, we were fortunate to have a high degree of symmetry and cultural alignment. Some of our differences were subtle or involved the language each organization used to describe a process. For example, we now refer to our performance huddles, which we conducted as a part of TOPS (the One Medical Performance System), as "business reviews"—in keeping with Amazon's terminology. We also follow their processes and documentation guidelines for those reviews. Conversely, Amazon Health Services has formally adopted and implemented C-I-CARE as a customer service methodology.

Industry watchers, healthcare experts, and some One Medical members have talked to me "off the record" about their guarded optimism and concerns about the long-term successful integration of the One Medical and Amazon cultures. One described Amazon as "a machine" and One Medical "as a human" and asked whether the "soul of One Medical will remain over the years." Others have questioned whether Amazon will uphold One Medical's privacy and personal service standards. Yet others wonder if Amazon will sustain a commitment to the importance of human service providers and in-person care. Some are concerned about Amazon "corporatizing" One Medical by taking a "you will do everything our way" approach to healthcare service delivery.

While acknowledging these concerns, Christine is optimistic about successful cultural integration:

> I believed Neil Lindsay when he told me he was a fan of One Medical and our culture. He was a member long before the acquisition and is passionate about wellness. We had many conversations about culture and what makes One Medical's culture special. He has committed to me that he wants to ensure the "heart" of what we deliver remains the same.
>
> Of course, we will adopt Amazon's Leadership Principles and develop our own tenets, keeping our human-centered culture alive. We are aligned on important topics such as patient safety, privacy, and clinical outcomes so that part of the integration is seamless. He also understands that health services require an intimately personal and unyielding commitment to the skilled professionals who deliver the care. We are committed to making this integration capture the best of both companies.

Before we explore the Amazon Health Services vision, how One Medical fits into that vision, and the opportunities and challenges ahead for Amazon One Medical, let's take a moment to apply lessons from Amazon and One Medical's business integration to ensure you are Winning Through People & Technology.

### WINNING THROUGH PEOPLE & TECHNOLOGY

1. How well does your team, department, or organization sustain business momentum, maintain employee and customer engagement, make big decisions that drive efficiencies, and communicate effectively across your organization? What are your strengths and opportunities in these areas?

2. Has your company encountered workforce reductions? If so, how did layoffs affect your organization over the short and long term?

3. How does your organization's cultural framework compare with Amazon's mission, four principles, and 16 leadership principles? Contrast your business with Amazon from the perspective of guidance, inspiration, and practical value. Imagine blending your culture with Amazon. What elements of your culture would you most want to retain? What elements of Amazon's culture would you most welcome?

4. Given customers' "divine discontent"—where yesterday's invention is today's new normal—how well does your team, department, or organization seek to resolve that discontent by getting up each day driven to invent ways to make your customers' lives easier and better?

5. How has your team, department, or organization expedited movement through Tuckman's FSNP (forming, storming, norming, and performing) stages of team development? What have you done to organize team tasks, drive cohesion, share leadership, and ensure high performance?

## THINKING BIG

To support Amazon's overarching mission ("to be Earth's most customer-centric company, Earth's best employer, and Earth's safest place to work"),

Amazon Health Services has developed its own mission "to make it dramatically easier for customers/members/patients to find, choose, afford, and engage with everything they need to get and stay well."

To achieve Amazon Health Services' mission, leaders are leveraging on-demand visits, the One Medical primary care membership model, Health Condition Programs (HCPs), pharmacy services, and a Flexible Spending Account (FSA)/Health Savings Account (HSA) store. Starting in July 2024, Amazon Health Services took one of its product lines (formerly Amazon Clinic) and blended it with One Medical under the name Amazon One Medical. Amazon Clinic was introduced in 2023 as a way for patients to purchase care on demand. For example, a person without a One Medical membership could, for a set fee, receive immediate treatment for a condition like a urinary tract infection. Under the 2024 realignment, Amazon One Medical is the division of Amazon Health Services that offers both membership and pay-per-visit options.

At the time of this writing, Amazon One Medical's pay-per-visit option gives patients a choice between a one-time virtual "message visit" (priced at $29) or a "video visit" (priced at $49). The health.amazon.com website lists dozens of common conditions effectively treated through a virtual visit, such as:

- Acid reflux (GERD)
- Cold sores (oral herpes)
- Cough, cold, flu, and strep throat
- Depression prescription renewals
- Eczema
- Gout attack
- High cholesterol
- Joint and back pain
- Period cramp relief
- Pink eye (conjunctivitis)
- Rosacea
- Seasonal allergies
- Stomach issues

When patients click "Pay-per-visit" on the Amazon Health Services website, they are asked to choose the condition for which they seek care and the state where they are located. They are then given the option of text "messaging" or "video visit" along with the price for each option and when a provider is available (e.g., $29 message only—response time from four hours, or $49 video—wait time from one hour). The patient then answers relevant medical questions and connects with the provider through the method they selected. The provider offers a medically appropriate treatment plan and sends any required prescriptions to the pharmacy of the patient's choice. As part of the virtual visit, the patient is provided an opportunity to message or video chat with their provider about the condition for which they are being treated. After receiving their treatment plan, patients can continue to message their provider for up to 14 days as follow-up to that condition.

By contrast, the Amazon One Medical membership option gives patients access to the traditional "One Medical" model established before the Amazon acquisition. At the time of this writing, the health.amazon .com website presents the Amazon One Medical membership value proposition as a 45% savings to Prime members ($9 a month or $99 per year), which provides access to:

- 24/7 on-demand care via VideoChat or Treat Me Now
- In-app health records and care plans
- Secure messaging with a provider
- Convenient prescription refills and renewal requests

The site also notes that membership enables individuals to:

Book billable in-person Office Visits or virtual Remote Visits in states where we have offices.

- **Office Visits:** Scheduled, in-office appointments with your primary care provider or a provider of your choice that are billed to you/your insurance. Copays and deductibles apply when billed to insurance.
- **Remote Visits:** Scheduled, virtual appointments with your primary care provider or a provider of your choice that are

billed to you/your insurance. Copays and deductibles apply
when billed to insurance.

Prime members also can add up to five additional memberships for $6
per person per month.

Amazon's Health Condition Programs (HCPs) are designed to help
patients with medical issues that require management, such as high blood
pressure, pre-diabetes, obesity, or type 1 or type 2 diabetes. When individuals with these types of conditions visit the Amazon Health Services
site, they can determine if they qualify for HCP's zero-dollar out-of-pocket
programs through their employer or insurance provider. Qualified patients
can then apply and, if accepted, receive an appropriate health monitoring
device (e.g., a continuous glucose monitor—CGM) and 24/7 messaging
access to a "virtual-first" care team that will coach and support the patient
toward their maintenance goals.

Amazon Pharmacy launched in 2020 as an evolution of Amazon's 2018
acquisition of PillPack. PillPack, a part of the current Amazon Pharmacy
offerings, packages prescriptions, over-the-counter (OTC) medications, and
vitamins into easy-to-manage and readily opened packets. PillPack ships
those packets to patients along with other healthcare items like creams, testing supplies, and inhalers. PillPack resolves issues with insurance providers, manages refills, and adjusts prescriptions if they change. More broadly,
Amazon Pharmacy is a prescription fulfillment service available to anyone
who signs up at pharmacy.amazon.com. The fundamental value proposition for Amazon Pharmacy is:

- Acceptance of most insurance
- Low prices, with or without insurance
- Upfront and transparent pricing
- Pharmacists on call 24/7
- Automatic refills, delivered to your door

In 2023, Amazon Pharmacy added a purchasable benefit called "RxPass
for Amazon Prime Members" available in most states. Since June 2024, that
benefit has been extended to both Medicare and non-Medicare patients.

This benefit provides "unlimited access to 60 eligible prescription medications for just $5 a month, plus fast, free delivery."

The final offering in Amazon Health Services' current suite of products and services is the Amazon Flexible Spending Account (FSA)/Health Savings Account (HSA) store. As you likely know, FSAs and HSAs are pre-tax accounts that fund healthcare expenses like copays, medical bills, and eligible health-related items. Amazon provides a learning center that answers questions about FSAs and HSAs. It also enables customers with pre-funded HSA/FSA cards to upload them to the Amazon site and use them like debit cards for qualifying purchases. Amazon has created an FSA/HSA store for qualifying items like vitamins and supplements, cold and allergy products, and digestive aids.

Neil Lindsay shares that AHS needs to continually innovate and scale to achieve its goals:

> Our mission is massive and unending. It is about choice, convenience, and ultimately enabling people to access the continuity of care they need and deserve. Our Amazon Health Service mission requires us to make it easy to get care, receive medication, and access everything people require to get and stay well. That involves ensuring there are more primary care locations to serve more patients. In parallel, we have to make virtual care experiences more complete so patients are less reliant on physical locations. These are ripe opportunities for us to scale and innovate by getting to more places at a lower cost while continually improving our outstanding experience. We must keep raising the bar and invent new ways to help people access care. All of that comes together through Amazon Health Services.

As noted by Neil, part of Amazon One Medical's challenge will be to ensure the company opens more physical "locations to serve more patients." For example, I live in Saint Petersburg, Florida, and the closest Amazon One Medical office is in Miami, which is roughly a four-hour drive. As an Amazon One Medical member, my primary membership benefits are

"Treat Me Now" messaging and on-demand virtual appointments. If I lived in Miami, I could see a One Medical primary care provider through my insurance and book a same- or next-day in-office or virtual appointment with that care team.

Historically, as shared in chapter 3, One Medical's process for opening clinics in a new city involved lengthy pre-work to secure a partnership with an established local healthcare system. To move at the speed of Amazon, One Medical leaders are reconceptualizing how they might rapidly provide broader access to in-person care as part of the Amazon One Medical membership. Amazon One Medical CEO Trent Green explains:

> Here's how we might extend our reach without having to build an office and recruit providers for every community in America. Let's assume you are a member in Bangor, Maine, where we don't have Amazon One Medical offices. We could go to health insurance carriers in Bangor, Maine; let's assume one of them is Anthem Blue Cross Blue Shield and forge connections with highly rated primary care providers in their network. We could work with providers from that group who are willing to provide insurance-reimbursable in-office services to our members living in Bangor while we provide virtual and after-hours care. The technology integration component might be a bit complicated, but identifying partners and crafting a win-win value proposition should not be difficult. This is just one of many innovative ways we are looking to expand our reach in innovative ways that benefit members and existing high-quality primary care providers.

Will Kimbrough, MD, is enthusiastic about supporting Neil Lindsay's vision of increasing physical clinics *and* reducing situations where members need to be seen in person. Will notes:

> I'm really optimistic about the future of virtual primary care. A few barriers have to be figured out, but, in general, the pandemic proved we can provide quality care virtually for issues we previously believed could only be addressed in an office. If you have the

technology to do a virtual visit (like our app), a home blood pressure cuff, and a lab facility within a reasonable driving distance, that should address about 85% of primary care issues. Typically, in-office practices like checking a patient's reflexes are primarily theater—unless that patient actually has a neurologic concern. Fortunately, we have seen significantly increased comfort levels with virtual care from patients and providers since the pandemic.

For Will, accelerating and widening virtual care use will require clinicians to continue to shift their perspective:

I have led all of our virtual teams, including the virtual medical team, and have heard the skepticism of some primary care providers regarding virtual care. Their concerns are reflected in questions like, "How can you tell a patient doesn't have pneumonia if you don't listen to their lungs?" My answer is, "Because they have a cold."

Realistically, we can't listen to the lungs of every person with a cold when they otherwise feel fine. So, our challenge will be determining when we need to be physically present to touch a patient. What are we gaining by palpating the thyroid, listening to a set of lungs, and pressing on a belly during a checkup? For most issues, we need to talk to patients, get laboratory information, and have access to pharmacies. Much of what we do may be little more than routine behaviors entrenched in historic practice patterns.

Andrew Diamond, MD, sees the need for expanded virtual care services as an imperative *not* just for Amazon Health Services but for healthcare across the United States:

Ultimately, some people will need most of their primary care to be done virtually. There are, and will continue to be, healthcare deserts in America. Given an emerging shortage of at least 100,000 primary care clinicians coupled with the needs of an aging population, we have to find ways to expand longitudinal primary care service virtually—knowing that people will intermittently need clinic visits for things like skin biopsies.

Amazon One Medical CEO Trent Green's vision for the future involves expanding to address the "healthcare deserts" Andrew referenced:

We are already among the country's largest integrated primary care groups—offering everything from pediatrics to geriatrics—but we want to continue to grow and develop. To date, One Medical has attracted and retained members through our ease of access and elevated service experience, and other competitors are catching up on those dimensions.

As part of Amazon, I want One Medical to impact the health of tens of millions of people and attract thousands of providers. I want to ensure providers experience ease and can live their purpose. I also want Amazon One Medical to leverage technologies that extend quality care efficiently.

Contrary to trends for condition-specific (point solutions), Trent wants to differentiate One Medical as a primary care service network that comprehensively meets member needs acutely and across their life span:

We are seeing a rise in point solution providers like Hims for hair loss, Maven for menopause, and Omada for diabetes. In some respects, the rise of these offerings reflects inadequate access to primary care—hair loss, clinical support for women in menopause, and diabetes management are entirely in the scope of practice for primary care providers. Amazon One Medical must continue expanding access to more people while maintaining our quality experiences, but we must also help people understand our comprehensiveness. Whether it's hair loss, menopause, or diabetes, we are a care organization first and foremost. We offer the care our patients want and need and leverage technology so they can receive it where they are.

We want people to come to One Medical to receive care for a specific condition but stay for broader care. We're spending a lot of time with our Amazon colleagues using large language models and AI as interpreters of maladies so we can help actively guide members to the right channel for what they need.

As part of Trent's goals to maximize the breadth and scope of Amazon One Medical's services, he is working to leverage Amazon's expansive offerings. Trent shares:

We are looking across the Amazon ecosystem and envisioning possibilities. For example, how might we integrate with Amazon Fresh to help you access nutritionally sound options if you are working on weight management? How might we leverage technologies like Alexa to check in and prompt clinical action concerning medication compliance or isolation for our senior population?

We are also leveraging Amazon's technology expertise to enhance our app. As a runner, assume I choose to share some data from my running app to the One Medical app. Further, assume my primary care provider knows how important daily running is to me. Now, imagine receiving a message from my provider through the One Medical app checking in on me because I haven't run in a couple of weeks. While these are only ideas, they highlight the exciting possibilities ahead.

In addition to increasing physical locations, innovating virtual solutions, and leveraging Amazon's vast resources, Amazon Health Services will also help Amazon One Medical manage costs. Neil Lindsay shares:

We understand the tension between customer experience and cost and constantly work to satisfy both elements. If you compromise the customer experience to lower costs, you likely will dilute the experience to the point it will fail. If we had a magic wand, we would make that tension disappear. However, in reality, we must first invent ways to make the provider's experience easier—so they can continue to offer outstanding patient experiences at scale. We are continuously pursuing technologies and tools like AI—so that providers can spend more time with patients and improve their experiences at lower costs.

As noted throughout the book, One Medical's leaders have been innovating solutions since the company's inception to help care teams reduce administrative tasks and increase quality time with patients. Allison Kroll, Senior Director of Product Management at One Medical, sees Amazon's technology assets as expediting solutions for providers.

Thanks to Amazon, we are taking on substantial provider challenges. For example, we are working on solutions that will help providers access the information they need in a relevant and manageable way. Historically, a primary care provider might receive hundreds of pages of documentation after a patient is discharged from an emergency department visit. We are working on machine learning to help our providers call out what they need in different scenarios so it can be highlighted for them. Our Chief Medical Officer, Andrew Diamond, likens the current state to an email box where all emails have the subject line labeled "email." We are making solid progress in helping our care providers find what they need when they want that information. I just participated in an article where the AMA studied this hurdle, noting that information management challenges have shifted from acquiring information to making meaning from all the available information.

Similarly, Group Product Manager Kyle Munkittrick shares how Amazon brings technology platforms to One Medical providers so they can gather and share information more effectively:

We've also worked to develop AI that summarizes clinical documents, saving providers time when prepping for appointments with new or existing patients. This technology extracts key clinical information from a patient's health record, distilling important themes and enabling providers to quickly digest information when preparing for a patient visit. Many One Medical PCPs regularly spend 5–10 minutes orienting to an unfamiliar chart before a 30-minute visit.

As it relates to the provider experience, Andrew Diamond, MD, notes:

I used to spend more than an hour every day painstakingly reviewing the results of diagnostic tests, notes from specialist visits and hospital stays, prior medical records, and more. Documents like that can run hundreds of pages long, and finding the signal in the noise can be next to impossible, especially at the end of a long day. But now, our technology puts a concise, accurate summary of the key events at the top of every document, saving me loads of time and focusing my attention on things that really matter.

From a patient/member perspective, Cassy Clouse, an Amazon One Medical Product Design Manager, envisions a future where Amazon product lines converge to drive a more integrated and easier healthcare experience:

Many ideas and actions are incubating to support an integrated care ecosystem. For example, in One Medical's electronic health record, providers can see if a medication is available for same-day or next-day delivery through Amazon Pharmacy. Since convenience is of higher importance than the price for many commercially insured patients, providers can decide when to advise patients that their medications can be delivered promptly through Amazon Pharmacy. I'm excited about how the Amazon partnership allows us to own and impact areas that improve patient outcomes. I imagine a future state where we make it easy and seamless for patients to get longitudinal primary care, access on-demand urgent care, receive prescriptions, and purchase other medically related items. Technological innovation and integration, coupled with compassionate and well-equipped providers, will ensure patients are seen quickly and have their prescriptions filled economically and effortlessly. It will also allow providers to know if a patient's prescription was filled and if their medication use pattern reflects adherence to the treatment plan. Providers could also help patients acquire FSA/HSA health-related products easily.

Before we look at how Amazon Health Services is pursuing both transformational and incremental improvements, let's take a moment to apply lessons from Amazon One Medical's diverse suite of services to ensure you are Winning Through People & Technology.

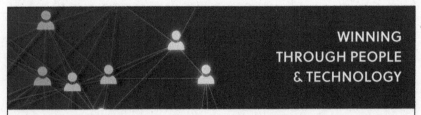

## WINNING THROUGH PEOPLE & TECHNOLOGY

1. How are you "thinking big" about your service offerings? What specifically are you aspiring to achieve through your people and technologies?

2. In what ways are you making "it dramatically easier for customers/members/patients to find, choose, afford, and engage with everything they need . . ."?

3. What entrenched behaviors or historical patterns (like Dr. Will Kimbrough's example of clinicians wanting to listen to every patient's lungs) get in the way of pursuing customer experience innovations? How might you effectively challenge those behaviors and patterns?

4. How are you navigating the tension of customer experience and cost? Where have you leaned too far into cost reduction and unduly compromised the customer experience? Conversely, where have you created elevated customer experiences that could be more affordable or sustainable?

5. Are AI, machine learning, and other technologies making the lives of your team members easier and more productive? If so, how does that translate into an improved customer experience? Where might you deploy more technologies to streamline the team member experience?

Neil Lindsay frames Amazon Health Services' innovation approach this way:

> Firstly, as I've mentioned, there are countless opportunities to make the provider experience easier and similar opportunities to make it easier for patients to receive care without leaving the convenience of their homes. There is also an incredible opportunity for innovation in diagnostics, treatments, and pharmaceuticals. Work is also needed to increase wellness and proactive healthcare to reduce chronic conditions.
>
> I am enthusiastic and impatient by the breadth of opportunities in healthcare and know the list extends beyond any company's capacity. The challenging question is often, what do we do next? We are constantly focused on that question, and we celebrate our teams and other companies who make it easier and cost-effective for customers and patients to get the quality healthcare they need.

While technology will likely play a dramatic role in the future of healthcare (and all business sectors, for that matter), Neil reminds us to pay attention to transformational *and* incremental improvements:

> I am excited by all the things that people are inventing in AI, robotics, and pharmaceuticals. Many of these represent big leaps forward, and we embrace those types of innovations as long as they prioritize patient safety and clinical outcomes.
>
> Since **today is day one at** Amazon, we are also looking to remove inconvenience and waste or streamline a process.
>
> Often, when I talk to large audiences, I'll ask people to imagine each of us addressing one "paper cut"—one thing we know is frustrating for customers. It may be a simple thing that has been low on our list of priorities, but imagine if we all looked for solutions to those types of patient or member frustrations. Now, imagine we did that every day and every month. Over time, healthcare would become dramatically easier.

QUICK
CHECKUP

What might your organization achieve if every person consistently looked for solutions to small things ("paper cuts") that are frustrating your customers?

One example of where Amazon Health Services has addressed a healthcare "paper cut" is the delivery of prescription medication through Amazon Pharmacy. Neil explains:

> Historically, patients could only visit a pharmacy to pick up a prescription medication. Typically, they had to stand in line to hand their prescription to a pharmacy team member. They would wander around the pharmacy for about 20 minutes before being called to complete their transaction. Finally, they would find out the price before receiving their medication. That process was unlike almost every retail transaction, where you know the price before going to the counter.
>
> To address that paper cut, we invented machine learning models that estimated the price range for medication and constantly refined our estimates. Ultimately, we needed the industry to feed the API all real-time data, but we couldn't wait for that to happen. So, we invented our solution to the paper cut.

Before we close out the book by using a One Medical member story to help you apply key insights on "human-centered/technology-powered" experience creation, let's take a moment to look at this chapter's Transformational Lessons.

# TRANSFORMATIONAL LESSONS

- Amazon's founder, Jeff Bezos, believes, "The most important single thing is to focus obsessively on the customer."
- Often, mergers and acquisitions are rich with promise and pain.
- Kison Patel suggests common post-acquisition challenges include maintaining employee and customer engagement, navigating senior leadership changes, addressing potential culture shifts, integrating technology systems, having the courage to make big decisions that drive expected efficiencies and capitalize on strengths, and communicating effectively within and across the newly merged organizations.
- Amazon pursues a mission ("to be Earth's most customer-centric company, Earth's best employer, and Earth's safest place to work") and operates from four core principles: (1) customer obsession rather than competitor focus, (2) passion for invention, (3) commitment to operational excellence, and (4) long-term thinking.
- Sixteen leadership principles reinforce Amazon's core principles. A few examples include "think big," "earn trust," "dive deep," and "deliver results."
- Amazon Health Services has an aspirational mission that supports Amazon's overarching mission. AHS's mission is "to make it dramatically easier for customers/members/patients to find, choose, afford, and engage with everything they need to get and stay well."
- To achieve its mission, Amazon Health Services combines on-demand visits, the One Medical primary care membership model, health condition programs (HCPs), pharmacy services, and a Flexible Spending Account/Health Savings Account store.
- Innovation requires people to be willing to challenge and give up historic behaviors and patterns.

- There is an inherent tension between customer experience and cost, and successful organizations constantly work to satisfy both.
- Given customers' divine discontent—where yesterday's invention is today's new normal—Amazon embraces that discontent with a "day one" mindset—where every day, people get up to create solutions that make customers' lives better.
- Breakthrough technologies like AI and machine learning should serve team members and customers. By automating tasks, team members should have more capacity to serve customers.
- While breakthrough technologies should be explored and embraced in the context of customer safety and outcomes, incremental improvement opportunities also pay significant dividends over time.
- Irrespective of industry, encouraging every team member to look for ways to remove customer inconvenience ("paper cuts") is integral to a culture of innovation and customer experience enhancement.

## CHAPTER 8

# What About You?

The purpose of business is to create
and keep a customer.

*Peter Drucker, management
consultant and author*[1]

I started this book with a warning—suggesting you only read it if you are committed to creating value through a human-centric and technology-powered approach for your customers (and other stakeholders in your service experience ecosystem). Your willingness to journey this far reflects a dedication to learning. So, let's build on your passion for experiential excellence through a story that calls you to act in ways that will further attract, serve, and retain internal and external customers.

The story is based on a patient whom I will call Mark and the countless Amazon One Medical team members who have cared for him. Mark, a then 31-year-old professional working in San Francisco, describes his healthcare journey by noting:

I was young, healthy, and fit. I wasn't very familiar with the medical system and had only rarely seen a doctor over the years when something like a foot injury popped up. In 2014, my partner at the time began telling me that I froze, kicked, and gasped in my sleep. I assumed those symptoms were brought on by working in the high-stress technology industry, so I didn't seek treatment. Unfortunately, later that year, I had a seizure while visiting my family in a small northern Arizona town and had to be admitted to a regional hospital. During my stay, a CT scan revealed an abnormal result, so they followed it with an MRI. I will never forget when the doctor came to my room to discuss the MRI results. I was sitting with my mom next to me. In a matter-of-fact voice lacking compassion, the doctor said, "A brain tumor caused your seizure." I became hyper-focused on his words and responded, "Oh my God, wait, what?" He simply restated his original words, so I had to probe for context. "What does that mean for me? What's the prognosis? Where do I go from here?" To which he literally said, "These things don't usually turn out well. You probably have six to twelve months to live."

My mother started crying, and I was reeling from his response, which lacked humanity and changed my life.

The author of *Emotional Intelligence*, Daniel Goleman, suggests, "True compassion means not only feeling another's pain but also being moved to help relieve it."

People contact you, your team, your department, or your organization to resolve underlying needs. In healthcare, those needs typically involve receiving a diagnosis, increasing function, curing a disease, or alleviating suffering. In other business settings, those needs might be the tangible benefits of your products or emotional and experiential factors like peace of mind, enjoyment, or escape. Irrespective of your business, most people don't come to you solely because they want you to be kind and compassionate. They come so you will resolve their problem. **However, they stay with you when you meet their needs with empathy and demonstrate authentic care for them.**

Mark's attending physician and the regional hospital addressed his need for a medical diagnosis *but* failed to deliver compassionate and human-centered care.

## YOUR CALL TO ACTION

- Take a moment to think about the underlying needs of your colleagues and customers.
- What percentage of the time do you meet those needs?
- What percentage of the time do you deliver your solutions empathetically and compassionately?
- If your answer to either of those questions is less than 100%, what training, processes, or systems will you start putting in place immediately to ensure compassionate need fulfillment?

The day after Mark received his cataclysmic diagnosis, he was transferred to a neurological institute in Phoenix.

I was in the care of specialists who were realistic but encouraging. They offered me options and a prognosis that wasn't as bleak as it had been presented the day before. My neurosurgeon talked about having many more years ahead of me and focused on the quality of my life. He was skilled and equipped to talk about my specific situation, and he did so from a caring yet evidence-based perspective. I had hope and, within 72 hours, was undergoing brain surgery.

The stark difference between my two healthcare experiences in Arizona made me more discerning about who I wanted to support me from a primary care perspective. When I returned to San Francisco about a month after my brain surgery, I knew I didn't want to be seen by the provider who had treated me intermittently before the tumor. We didn't have a relationship, and he was primarily focused on getting me in and out of his office with a prescription. He was not the person I wanted to help me navigate my post-surgery recovery.

Mark heard about One Medical from his work colleagues. They described their primary care membership experience as personal, relational, high quality, convenient, and tech forward. Mark supplemented those word-of-mouth recommendations with online research. Based on his due diligence, he signed up for a One Medical membership and downloaded the app.

As noted in chapter 2, Amazon founder Jeff Bezos said, "Your brand is what other people say about you when you're not in the room."

The experiences you provide to your team members and customers are discussed with their friends and associates and shared online with countless strangers.

When Mark determined that his existing relationship with his primary care provider was transactional, he looked for alternatives through his friends and online searches. Those sources converged to describe the "lived experience" of members in the context of One Medical's human-centric (personal, relational, high quality) and technology-powered (convenient and tech-forward) strengths.

What do you want colleagues and/or customers to say about you and your business when you aren't in the room?

What are you and your team members doing to increase the likelihood of people saying what you hope to hear?

To what degree are colleagues and customers sharing your desired words in social media posts or surveys?

How do you leverage formal and informal listening to ensure online reviews and referrals differentiate you from the competition?

**YOUR CALL TO ACTION**

- Write down a description of your optimal team member or customer experience.
- Listen to peers and customers (formally and informally) to determine the degree to which they talk about your brand in the ways you desire.
- Use what you hear to improve the experience and keep listening to ensure your improvements resonate.
- Set goals and track the number of people who visit your business through referrals.
- Ask customers how they came to know about you and what they heard about you and your brand.

Upon downloading the One Medical app, Mark found it easy to use to select a provider and schedule an initial appointment. Arriving for his initial appointment, Mark was greeted immediately and warmly in a setting he described as "warm, contemporary, and inviting." May Lin, DO, walked him to a treatment room for his on-time appointment. Mark was struck by how Dr. Lin listened attentively and provided a safe and unrushed space for him to discuss his recent medical challenges. He valued her knowledge, respectfulness, and kindness. It would begin a long and rewarding professional relationship for Mark and Dr. May Lin.

Will Rogers once said, "You never get a second chance to make a first impression."

Similarly, my friend and leadership author Mark Sanborn believes "what starts bad often gets worse."

These quotes capture the importance of deploying people and technology to ensure that colleagues and customers have positive initial experiences. On the people side, internal research conducted at AT&T retail stores shows customers decide whether to stay or leave within 10 seconds of arrival. Customers not greeted within that short time are significantly more likely to turn and go. Princeton researchers have found that decisions about attractiveness, likability, trustworthiness, competence, and aggression are made within one-tenth of a second. First impressions do matter, and customers expect to be greeted promptly.

Poor initial technology experiences also contribute to customer churn. A Super Monitoring study showed that 57% of users aren't willing to recommend a business with a poorly designed mobile site.[2] If your website isn't mobile friendly, that first impression sends customers away and decreases the likelihood they will refer friends, colleagues, and family to your business.

In Mark's case, technology made administrative tasks easy, and One Medical's people welcomed him swiftly and warmly.

What do you want colleagues and/or customers to sense and feel when they first interact with your technology or people?

What are they actually seeing, tasting, touching, hearing, smelling, and feeling?

To what degree have you studied the arrival moments of prospective team members and customers across all interactional channels (e.g., email, phone, in person, live chat, chatbots)?

Are all those arrival experiences setting your team members or clients on a firm foundation with you and your company?

**YOUR CALL TO ACTION**

- List the channels through which you interact with prospective team members or customers.
- Identify the arrival moments for customers across each channel.

- Use a tool like an empathy map (*see figure below*) to study arrival experiences based on varied need states and employee/customer segments.
- Look for opportunities to greet and drive a consistently elevated multi-sensory arrival experience.
- Explore ways to remove elements of the welcoming experiences that get in the way of forming an initial connection (e.g., unhelpful signage or unnecessary app features).
- Repeat the empathy mapping process for other high-value moments (outlined in chapter 4), such as transitions, pain points, and departures.

# Empathy Map

Through his years as a member, Mark experienced continuous improvements in the customer-facing app and found value in how it enabled him to communicate efficiently with May. He also used the app for "Treat Me Now" text messaging and, as needed, for visits with the virtual care team.

The President of 92Y, Stuart J. Ellman, noted, "Social media and technology are *not* agents of change. They are just tools. We, the connected people, are the agents of change."

For Amazon One Medical members like Mark, technologies like the app are tools for human connection. For One Medical technology designers and developers, the app and the electronic health record are ways to make the patient and provider experience more accessible and navigable. By applying thoughtful yet rapid design, One Medical team members support many of Amazon's leadership principles (listed in chapter 7), including diving deep, having a bias for action, and delivering results.

**YOUR CALL TO ACTION**

- Audit your technologies to ensure they connect people to your products and services, reduce your team members' effort, and/ or drive customer convenience.
- Assess your approach to technological and human experience design, ensuring it follows design best practices (provided in chapter 4) and supports a culture of continuous improvement.
- Ensure you are leveraging technology as a tool for human connection rather than a replacement for personal contact.

In addition to receiving intermittent care from the virtual care team, Mark was seen by other care providers in May's office when she was unavailable. Mark shares the extreme importance of One Medical's collaborative care approach, given a dramatic shift in his condition:

I had worked closely with Dr. May Lin for six years, and she played a pivotal role in helping me navigate and emotionally cope with my recovery from the brain surgery. I knew she was about to scale back her clinical practice to pursue an academic position, and I was happy for her. While I'd developed a solid relationship with her, I felt I could transition to another One Medical provider and develop a positive relationship with them.

My trust in One Medical was based on my interactions with other providers through the years. For example, I saw other clinicians when May was on maternity leave. One Medical made my transition easy. They hire outstanding providers and ensure all relevant parties have access to my records—so it didn't feel like I was starting over. Also, May was still on staff at One Medical, which meant I could message her if needed.

Thank goodness the transition was swift and successful because, around the time I changed doctors, my brain tumor recurred.

---

Basketball superstar Michael Jordan noted, "Talent wins games, but teamwork and intelligence win championships."

Mark recognized One Medical's ability to attract highly qualified and compassionate professionals. He also acknowledged how those professionals, along with One Medical's systems (e.g., virtual care teams, in-office teams, and an effectively integrated electronic health record), fostered collaboration and a smooth transition during his time of crisis.

**YOUR CALL TO ACTION**

- Review One Medical's systematic process for selecting team members outlined in chapter 2.
- Compare and elevate your process for assessing prospects' technical and interpersonal competencies.

- Ensure you select people who will enhance your culture and continually seek to drive an awareness of your mission and values through onboarding.
- Much like One Medical's commitment to team member growth (outlined in chapter 6), continually develop your people's technical, collaborative, and leadership skills.
- Ask customers to evaluate the individual and collaborative performance of team members. For example, "How likely are you to recommend Susan?" and "How likely are you to recommend our team/division/organization?"

With the recurrence of his brain tumor, Mark required another surgery, radiation, and chemotherapy, which was provided at the University of California, San Francisco Medical Center (UCSF)—a One Medical healthcare partner. Mark praised the care he received at UCSF and recognized the seamless coordination between UCSF specialists and his One Medical primary care team. Through his successful recovery, Mark continued to praise the care he received across One Medical. He also adopted a more mobile lifestyle (increasing the value of accessing One Medical clinics across the United States). Mark encourages others to become Amazon One Medical members and extends compassion and healthcare knowledge to others:

As a cancer survivor, I've chosen to focus more on experiences and increase the time I spend with the people and places I love.

I gave up my apartment and built a little minivan camper with a couch that folds into a full-size bed. My camper has ample water, a fridge, and a solar-powered roof shower.

I've also needed to stay connected to the survivorship community. Unfortunately, when it comes to brain tumors, there wasn't a community specifically tailored to young adults. So, a couple of other young brain tumor survivors and I launched a support group that UCSF sponsors. I am honored to facilitate that group, attended by people from across the United States and multiple countries. The group helps participants cope with questions like, "How do I approach family, career, or retirement planning when I might die in six months?"

These days, I get a brain scan every four months, and each clean scan gives me a new lease on life. I view May as a friend and a continued part of my healthcare journey. I cannot tell you how refreshing or important she is to me. My primary care journey is in stark contrast to what I see happening to friends and support group members who are victims of a broken medical system.

To appreciate the reciprocal impact of Mark and Dr. Lin's relationship, I asked Mark for permission to talk to Dr. Lin. With his approval, she shared:

Mark is a special person who faces a severe diagnosis that is uncommon in younger populations. While he entered my office with considerable positivity, he had been through a lot, starting with the way he received his diagnosis.

In primary care, I often find myself trying to help people move past wounds from the healthcare system so they can remain motivated and advocate for themselves. My goal during Mark's first visit was to help him gain enough trust to return for subsequent visits. Our relationship over the years reinforces my reason for going into primary care.

I've had the privilege of having longstanding trust-based relationships with Mark and many other patients. As part of that trust, people talk to me about things they might hesitate to share with their closest family members.

What an incredible honor it's been to have helped Mark move forward in his care. Because of our relationship, Mark has asked questions, discussed concerns, addressed setbacks, and celebrated successes related to interactions with surgeons and other specialists. I sought to be his healthcare home base as he extended trust to other care providers.

I am very proud of and impressed by Mark's work to expand his impact on the lives of others. Over the years at One Medical, I've been encouraged to broaden my leadership and mentorship impact. For example, I became the Medical Director of One Medical's Emerging Leader Program and National Clinical Leader. I've also been able to maintain a clinical role at One Medical as I help the next generation of osteopathic physicians learn and grow through my role as the Assistant Dean of GME & Program Development for the Touro University California College of Osteopathic Medicine.

---

Albert Schweitzer opined, "The purpose of human life is to serve and show compassion and the will to help others."

May and Mark have helped each other and broadly extended their commitment to service others. Through their service, Mark and May find meaning and are making the world a better place.

**YOUR FINAL CALL TO ACTION**

- Consider and help colleagues reflect on the direct impact of service.
- Take one step further and consider how your impact extends beyond the people you directly serve. Think about how your service cascades through the people you serve to those they love, care for, and serve.
- Develop leadership and mentorship programs (like Amazon One Medical's emerging leader program, reviewed in chapter 6) that encourage people to broaden their service impact.
- In the spirit of Amazon's "day one" concept (highlighted in chapter 7), strive to wake up each morning to be of service by making the lives of your customers and colleagues easier and better.
- **Most importantly, don't forget to be grateful for the privilege of being of service.**

Given the importance of gratitude and "ending moments" in a customer's journey, thank you, my customer, for the time you've invested to read and learn about transformative lessons on service, innovation, and sustainability from Amazon One Medical.

More importantly, I hope you will share these lessons with others so that collectively, we will create extraordinary human-centered and technology-powered experiences that drive loyalty and referrals.

By "advancing confidently" in pursuit of elevated human experiences, I am certain (in the words of Henry David Thoreau) you will "meet with a success unexpected in common hours."

Thank you,
Joseph

# ACKNOWLEDGMENTS

The British author and journalist Tahir Shah wrote that "stories are a communal currency of humanity."

*All Business Is Personal* results from countless people sharing their humanity, wisdom, insights, and compassion so you, part of a community of readers and leaders, can learn, grow, and elevate human experiences. Since those storytellers have been referenced throughout the book, I will not list their names here. Instead, I will briefly highlight a handful of individuals who played a herculean role in humanizing One Medical and ensuring this story was told—starting with the soul of the brand and the lifeblood of this project, Chief People Officer Christine Morehead.

For context, I've been fortunate to have decades of experience working with extraordinary leaders across sectors and continents. Against that backdrop, Christine is unmatched in her genuine care for people, passion for servant leadership, and attention to detail. Not surprisingly, the One Medical team members that Christine assembled to support this project (Joanne Helms, Mollie Braaten, Pam Hubbuck, and others) also demonstrated exceptional professionalism and flawless support. Similarly, I owe a debt of gratitude to the individual who introduced me to One Medical and trusted me to play a consultative role in its customer/member experience journey—Amir Dan Rubin.

As noted in Amir's foreword, I had the privilege of working for and with him at UCLA as a patient experience consultant and author of *Prescription for Excellence* when Amir was UCLA Health System's Chief Operating Officer. Having watched Amir play a transformative role in two starkly different healthcare systems, I am awestruck by his intellect, strategic vision, commitment to operational excellence, authenticity, and kindness.

Of course, One Medical wouldn't exist without Dr. Tom Lee. I see Tom as a rebel described in Apple's 1990 "Think Different" campaign:

> Here's to . . . the rebels . . . the ones who see things differently . . .
> You can praise them, disagree with them, quote them, disbelieve
> them, glorify or vilify them. About the only thing you can't do is
> ignore them. Because they change things. They invent. They imagine. They heal. They explore. They create. They inspire. They push
> the human race forward.

Special thanks go to Neil Lindsay, Senior Vice President of Amazon Health Services, and Trent Green, Chief Executive Officer of One Medical, for being generous with their time, sharing their strategic perspectives, and enabling me to tell this story freely. I am also grateful to Victoria Zhou, Vice President and Assistant General Counsel of One Medical, for helping ensure the accuracy of the information I've provided, and to Andrew Diamond, MD, One Medical's Chief Medical Officer, who has spent considerable time through the years showing me what it means to be a compassionate clinician.

I also extend gratitude to Matt Holt, Editor-in-Chief of his imprint at BenBella Books, and his highly talented team that includes but is not limited to Katie Dickman, Lydia Choi, Jessika Rieck, Ariel Jewett, Brigid Pearson, and Mallory Hyde.

My wife, Patti, who sadly is accustomed to being acknowledged last, is a primary and unrelenting force behind this book (and most blessings in my life). From a practical perspective, she scheduled interviews, secured releases, proofed drafts, re-read drafts, and kept the book moving forward. On an emotional level, she listened to my challenges, accepted my unavailability during intensive writing, and worked tirelessly to create a warm and loving home for our entire family—our children Joseph "Andrew," Fiona,

Jessica, Matt, Andrew's wife (Leah), Matt's wife (Megan), and our grandchildren (Penelope, Lucy, Daniel, Emma, Michael, Brigham, Gracie, Robert, and Hailey). Thanks to all of them for supporting me—so I can share this (and my other business stories) with the person I hold in the highest esteem—*you*, the reader.

I am grateful that you spent your money and time reading *All Business Is Personal*. My gratitude is also a wish in keeping with Dr. Seuss's words: "The more that you read, the more things you will know. The more that you learn, the more places you'll go."

I hope the time you spent reading this book helps you continue to go places that make the world kinder and more caring and your life more prosperous and fulfilled.

# NOTES

## CHAPTER 1

Peter F. Drucker, quoted by Jeff Sore, "These 10 Peter Drucker Quotes May Change Your World," NBC News, September 16, 2014, www .nbcnews.com/id/wbna56060818.

2. The White House, "Using Technology to Improve Customer Experience and Service Delivery for the American People," Office of Management and Budget, December 13, 2021, www.whitehouse.gov/omb/briefing -room/2021/12/13/using-technology-to-improve-customer-experience -and-service-delivery-for-the-american-people/.

3. Patrick Forth, Tom Reichert, Romain de Laubier, and Saibal Chakraborty, "Flipping the Odds of Digital Transformation Success," Boston Consulting Group, October 29, 2020, www.bcg.com/publications/2020 /increasing-odds-of-success-in-digital-transformation.

4. Leah Leachman and Don Scheibenreif, "Using Technology to Create a Better Customer Experience," *Harvard Business Review*, March 17, 2023, hbr.org/2023/03/using-technology-to-create-a-better-customer -experience.

5. eHealthInsurance and Forrester Research, "The Cost and Benefits of Individual Health Insurance Plans" (Report, September 2007), www.ehealthinsurance.com/content/expertcenterNew/CostBenefits ReportSeptember2007.pdf.

6.  Physicians Foundation, "2018 Survey of America's Physicians: Practice Patterns and Perspectives" (Survey, September 2018), physicians foundation.org/wp-content/uploads/2018/09/physicians-survey-results -final-2018.pdf.

7.  David Rook, "A Brief History of Employer-Sponsored Healthcare," *Hub* (blog), August 27, 2020, www.griffinbenefits.com/blog/history-of -employer-sponsored-healthcare.

8.  One Medical internal data primary research, reduction of median GAD-7 scores for members who participated in Wellness Series.

9.  One Medical Member Satisfaction Survey, 2019.

10. CareFirst PCMH Ranking of Overall Performance Report, 2018.

11. One Medical Press Release, July 19, 2017.

12. 1Life Healthcare, "1Life Healthcare (One Medical) Announces Pricing of Initial Public Offering," GlobeNewswire, January 30, 2020, www.globe newswire.com/news-release/2020/01/31/1977884/0/en/1Life-Healthcare -One-Medical-Announces-Pricing-of-Initial-Public-Offering.html.

13. Yuechen Zhao, "One Medical, A History," *Medium* (blog), September 24, 2023, medium.com/@yuechenzhao/one-medical-a-history-69ee93e20dcd.

14. Michelle Davis, "One Medical Considers Options After Getting Takeover Interest," *Bloomberg*, July 5, 2022, www.bloomberg.com /news/articles/2022-07-05/one-medical-is-said-to-consider-options-after -takeover-interest.

15. Andy Jassy, quoted in "One Medical Joins Amazon to Make It Easier for People to Get and Stay Healthier," One Medical Media Center, February 22, 2023, www.onemedical.com/mediacenter/one-medical-joins -amazon/.

16. Jamie Ducharme, "Trent Green: Time100 Health 2024," *Time*, May 2, 2024, time.com/6963674/trent-green/.

## CHAPTER 2

1.  Edward Albert, quoted in "Edward Albert Quotes," Goodreads, www .goodreads.com/author/quotes/1652127.Edward_Albert.

2.  Purchaser Business Group on Health, "Using Primary Care's Potential to Improve Health Outcomes," PBGH, October 4, 2021, www.pbgh.org/using-primary-cares-potential-to-improve-health-outcomes/.

3.  National Association of Community Health Centers, "Closing the Primary Care Gap" (Report, February 2023), 3, www.nachc.org/wp-content/uploads/2023/06/Closing-the-Primary-Care-Gap_Full-Report_2023_digital-final.pdf.

4.  American Medical Association, "Doctor Shortages Are Here—and They'll Get Worse If We Don't Act Fast," AMA, April 13, 2022, www.ama-assn.org/practice-management/sustainability/doctor-shortages-are-here-and-they-ll-get-worse-if-we-don-t-act.

5.  Athenahealth, "Almost All U.S. Physicians Surveyed Feel Burned Out on a Regular Basis," Athenahealth, February 21, 2024, www.athenahealth.com/press-releases/us-physicians-surveyed-feel-burned-out-on-a-regular-basis.

6.  Sunita Mishra, "America Faces a Shortage of Primary Care Doctors—and They're Drowning in Work. Here's How AI Can Solve the Physician Burnout Crisis," *Fortune*, February 14, 2024, fortune.com/2024/02/14/america-shortage-primary-care-doctors-work-ai-physician-burnout-crisis/.

7.  Fatema Akbar, Gloria Mark, E. Margaret Warton, et al., "Physicians' Electronic Inbox Work Patterns and Factors Associated with High Inbox Work Duration," *Journal of the American Medical Informatics Association* 28, no. 5 (2021): 923–930, academic.oup.com/jamia/article/28/5/923/5924604.

8.  Deloitte, "2023 Gen Z and Millennial Survey," Deloitte, www2.deloitte.com/cn/en/pages/about-deloitte/articles/genzmillennialsurvey-2023.html.

9.  Ed O'Boyle, "4 Things Gen Z and Millennials Expect from Their Workplace," Gallup, March 30, 2021, www.gallup.com/workplace/336275/things-gen-millennials-expect-workplace.aspx.

10. Grant Olsen, "Why Do Businesses Fail?" Foundr, February 22, 2022, foundr.com/articles/building-a-business/why-do-businesses-fail.

11.  Anne Kadet, "Sabbaticals Are Companies' Latest Weapon Against the Great Resignation," *Fortune*, March 15, 2022, fortune.com/2022/03/15/sabbaticals-great-resignation-employee-benefit-perk/.

12.  Vijay Eswaran, "The Business Case for Diversity in the Workplace Is Now Overwhelming," World Economic Forum, April 29, 2019, www.weforum.org/agenda/2019/04/business-case-for-diversity-in-the-workplace/.

13.  Boston Consulting Group, "How Diverse Leadership Teams Boost Innovation," BCG, January 23, 2018, www.bcg.com/publications/2018/how-diverse-leadership-teams-boost-innovation.

14.  Dame Vivian Hunt et al., "Diversity Matters Even More: The Case for Holistic Impact," McKinsey & Company, December 5, 2023, www.mckinsey.com/featured-insights/diversity-and-inclusion/diversity-matters-even-more-the-case-for-holistic-impact.

15.  Ed O'Boyle, "4 Things Gen Z and Millennials Expect From Their Workplace."

16.  John E. Snyder et al., "Black Representation in the Primary Care Physician Workforce and Its Association With Population Life Expectancy and Mortality Rates in the US," *JAMA Network Open* 6, no. 4 (2023): e23 6687, jamanetwork.com/journals/jamanetworkopen/fullarticle/2803898.

17.  Revenue, Inc., "The Process for Effective Sales Execution," *Revenue, Inc.* (blog), www.revenue-inc.com/blog/sales-execution/.

18.  Jonnathan Coleman, "Healthcare Turnover Rates [2024 Update]," DailyPay (blog, accessed October 27, 2024), www.dailypay.com/resource-center/blog/employee-turnover-rates-in-the-healthcare-industry/.

## CHAPTER 3

1.  Don Tapscott, quoted in "Don Tapscott Quotes," AZ Quotes, www.azquotes.com/quote/1012356.

2.  Will Kenton, "Value Networks: Definitions, Benefits, and Types," Investopedia, December 19, 2022, www.investopedia.com/terms/v/value-network.asp.

3. Kaiser Family Foundation, "2023 Employer Health Benefits Survey," KFF, www.kff.org/health-costs/report/2023-employer-health-benefits -survey/.

4. Tina Reed, "Facing Higher Health Costs, Employers Get Tough," Axios, September 19, 2023, www.axios.com/2023/09/19/employers-benefits -insurer-negotiation.

5. Sanjay Basu et al., "Utilization and Cost of an Employer-Sponsored Comprehensive Primary Care Delivery Model," *JAMA Network Open* 4, no. 5 (2020): e203803, jamanetwork.com/journals/jamanetworkopen /fullarticle/2765201.

6. One Medical, "Virtual Visit FAQ," UnitedHealthcare, https://web .archive.org/web/20211021181837/https://www.myuhc.com/content /myuhc/Member/Assets/Pdfs/16-0271_JPMC_Virtual_Visit_FAQ _flyer_LowRes%2010.pdf; Kristin N. Ray et al., "Opportunity Costs of Ambulatory Medical Care in the United States," *American Journal of Managed Care* 21, no. 8 (2015): 567–574, https://pmc.ncbi.nlm.nih.gov /articles/PMC8085714; CDC, "Median Emergency Department (ED) Wait and Treatment Times, by Triage Level," CDC QuickStats, 2010– 2011, https://www.cdc.gov/mmwr/preview/mmwrhtml/mm6319a8.htm.

7. Substance Abuse and Mental Health Services Administration, "Key Substance Use and Mental Health Indicators in the United States: Results from the 2022 National Survey on Drug Use and Health" (Report, November 2023), 5–6, www.samhsa.gov/data/sites/default/files/reports /rpt42731/2022-nsduh-nnr.pdf.

8. Anxiety and Depression Association of America, "Anxiety Disorders— Facts & Statistics," ADAA, October 28, 2022, adaa.org/understanding -anxiety/facts-statistics.

9. George Petras, "2 US Suicide Rate Reaches Highest Point in More than 80 Years: See What Latest Data Shows," *USA Today*, November 29, 2023, www.usatoday.com/story/graphics/2023/11/29/2022-suicide-rate -historical-chart-comparison-graphic/71737857007/.

10. National Alliance on Mental Illness, "Mental Health By the Numbers," NAMI, April 2023, www.nami.org/about-mental-illness/mental-health -by-the-numbers/.

11. "Navigating the Deferred Care Crisis," One Medical, https://go .onemedical.com/report-navigating-the-deferred-care-crisis; "Why Employers Should Prioritize Healthcare to Attract and Retain Talent," Workplace Intelligence, https://newsletter.workplaceintelligence.com /posts/workplace-intelligence-insider-why-employers-should-prioritize -healthcare-to-attract-and-retain-talent.

12. Jim Harter, "US Engagement Hits 11-Year Low," Gallup, April 10, 2024, www.gallup.com/workplace/643286/engagement-hits-11-year-low.aspx.

13. Angie Howard, "Value-Based Care vs. Fee-for-Service," Medical Advantage, July 12, 2024, https://web.archive.org/web/20240723182146/https:// www.medicaladvantage.com/blog/value-based-care-vs-fee-for-service/.

14. Deloitte, "Equipping Physicians for Value-Based Care," Deloitte Insights, October 14, 2020, www2.deloitte.com/us/en/insights/industry /health-care/physicians-guide-value-based-care-trends.html.

15. Ruth De Backer and Eileen Kelly Rinaudo, "Improving the Management of Complex Business Partnerships," McKinsey & Company, March 21, 2019, www.mckinsey.com/capabilities/strategy-and-corporate-finance/our -insights/improving-the-management-of-complex-business-partnerships.

16. Mass General Brigham, "Company Overview," LinkedIn, www.linkedin .com/company/mass-general-brigham/.

17. Alok A. Khorana et al., "Time to Initial Cancer Treatment in the United States and Association with Survival Over Time: An Observational Study," *PLOS One* 14, no. 4 (2019): e0213209, journals.plos.org/plosone /article?id=10.1371/journal.pone.0213209.

## CHAPTER 4

1. Albert Einstein, quoted in "Albert Einstein Quotes," Quotefancy, quotefancy.com/quote/762934/Albert-Einstein-The-best-design-is-the -simplest-one-that-works.

2. Tim Brown, quoted in "Tim Brown Quotes," AZ Quotes, www.azquotes .com/quote/677932.

3. Thomas J. Watson Jr., quoted "Good Design Is Good Business," Archipreneur, May 9, 2019, https://archipreneur.com/good-design-is-good -business/.

4.  Brian Reed, quoted in Himani Nakrani, "What's a Good Design Any-way?," Medium (blog), September 5, 2021, https://medium.com/design -bootcamp/whats-a-good-design-anyway-81a1109bd067.

5.  Guerric de Ternay, "Amazon Value Proposition," FourWeekMBA, February 3, 2024, https://fourweekmba.com/amazon-value-proposition/.

6.  Roy Penchansky and J. William Thomas, "The Concept of Access: Definition and Relationship to Consumer Satisfaction," *Medical Care* 19, no. 2 (1981): 127–140, www.unboundmedicine.com/medline/citation /7206846/The_concept_of_access:_definition_and_relationship_to _consumer_satisfaction.

7.  Catherine Cote, "A Guide to Employee Journey Mapping," Harvard Business School Online, Business Insights Blog, December 8, 2022, online.hbs.edu/blog/post/employee-journey-mapping.

8.  Kyruus, "2023 Care Access Benchmark Report for Provider Organizations," Kyruus, kyruushealth.com/resource/2023-care-access-benchmark -report-for-provider-organizations/.

9.  Matthew Dixon, Karen Freeman, and Nick Toman, "Stop Trying to Delight Your Customers," *Harvard Business Review*, July–August 2010, hbr.org/2010/07/stop-trying-to-delight-your-customers.

10. Mike Henry, "Integrated CX: The Complete Guide" InMoment (blog, accessed October 27, 2024), inmoment.com/blog/integrated-customer -experience/.

11. Susan Sherer, Chad Meyerhoefer, and Donald Levick, "Challenges to Aligning Coordination Technology with Organizations, People, and Processes in Healthcare," *Proceedings of the 50th Hawaii International Conference on System Sciences* (2017): 3537–3545, pdfs.semanticscholar .org/91aa/18f4c4fae4ed26e006d4f06959fbb12d7bd2.pdf.

12. Weber Shandwick and KRC Research, "The Great American Search for Healthcare Information" (Report, January 2023), cms.weber shandwick.com/wp-content/uploads/2023/01/Healthcare-Info-Search -Report.pdf.

13. Tomoyuki Kuroiwa et al., "The Potential of ChatGPT as a Self-Diagnostic Tool for Common Orthopedic Diseases: Exploratory Study," *Journal of Medical Internet Research* 25, no. 1 (2023): e47621, www .jmir.org/2023/1/e47621.

14. Anthony Yeung et al., "TikTok and Attention-Deficit-Hyperactivity Disorder: A Cross-Sectional Study of Social Media Content Quality," *The Canadian Journal of Psychiatry* 67, no. 12 (2023): 899–906, journals .sagepub.com/doi/10.1177/07067437221082854.

15. Emily May, "How Digital Health Apps Are Empowering Patients, Improving Outcomes, and Increasing Accessibility," Deloitte UK Health Blog, October 28, 2021, blogs.deloitte.co.uk/health/2021/10/how -digital-health-apps-are-empowering-patients-improving-outcomes-and -increasing-accessibility.html.

16. Qualtrics, "The Healthcare Pain Index 2019" (Report, November 2019), www.qualtrics.com/m/assets/wp-content/uploads/2019/11/Healthcare _PI_Report.pdf.

17. Martinkovic Milford Architects, "One Medical: A Revolution in Primary Care," Martinkovic Milford, www.martinkovicmilford.com/project/one -medical-group/.

18. Steve Jobs, quoted in Dave Wilson, "Ideas vs. Execution," *Medium* (blog), August 16, 2017, medium.com/provencfo/ideas-vs-execution-6e a6e9ce82ca.

## CHAPTER 5

1. Robin Sharma, quoted in Chuka Chiezie, "Ideas Without Execu- tion = Delusion—Robin Sharma," *Medium* (blog), October 4, 2021, chukachiezie.medium.com/ideas-without-execution-delusion-robin -sharma-b1b6cbaff312.

2. Gino Wickman, *Traction: Get a Grip on Your Business* (Kindle Edition, 2012), location 500 of 3717.

3. Amaia Noguera Lasa, Andrea Pedroni, Asmus Komm, and Simon Gal- lot Lavallée, "In the Spotlight: Performance Management That Puts Peo- ple First," McKinsey & Company, May 15, 2024, https://www.mckinsey .com/capabilities/people-and-organizational-performance/our-insights /in-the-spotlight-performance-management-that-puts-people-first.

4. Huron, "Attracting, Developing, and Retaining Talent Using Leadership Rounding," Huron Consulting Group, www.huronconsultinggroup.com /insights/attracting-developing-retaining-talent-leadership-rounding.

5. Timothy McLean, "The 3 Essentials of a Lean Visual Management Board," TXM Lean Solutions, txm.com/the-3-essentials-of-a-visual-management-board/.

6. Bain & Company, quoted in Aaron Carpenter, "What is a good Net Promoter Score?," Qualtrics, https://www.qualtrics.com/experience-management/customer/good-net-promoter-score/.

7. Sabrina Tessitore, "NPS Healthcare Guide: 25 Healthcare NPS Benchmarks & Industry Guide," CustomerGauge Experience Benchmarks, customergauge.com/benchmarks/blog/nps-healthcare-net-promoter-score-benchmarks.

## CHAPTER 6

1. Ellen Glasgow, quoted in Indeed, "88 Motivational Quotes on Growth to in Business to Inspire You," Indeed Career Guide, August 18, 2024, www.indeed.com/career-advice/career-development/quotes-on-growth-in-business.

2. Peter Senge, *The Fifth Discipline: The Art & Practice of The Learning Organization*, quoted in Eric Cohen, "The Fifth Discipline," Funderstanding (blog), April 26, 2011, funderstanding.com/blog/the-fifth-discipline/.

3. Scott Keller and Mary Meaney, "Attracting and Retaining the Right Talent," *McKinsey Quarterly*, November 24, 2017, www.mckinsey.com/capabilities/people-and-organizational-performance/our-insights/attracting-and-retaining-the-right-talent.

4. Zurich Insurance Company, "Grow Your People to Grow Your Business," Zurich North America Knowledge Hub, July 17, 2023, www.zurichna.com/knowledge/articles/2023/07/grow-your-people-to-grow-your-business.

5. Lital Marom, "How to Build a Culture of Learning," *Forbes*, April 7, 2022, https://www.forbes.com/councils/forbescoachescouncil/2022/04/06/how-to-build-a-culture-of-learning/.

6. Herminia Ibarra and Anne Scoular, "The Leader as Coach," *Harvard Business Review*, November 2019, hbr.org/2019/11/the-leader-as-coach.

7. One Medical, "One Medical Provides Family Medicine for All Ages," One Medical Services, www.onemedical.com/services/family-medicine/.

8.  Branding Elm, "Breaking Down One Medical's Results: How Their Branding Strategy Elevated the Perception of Medical Brands," LinkedIn Pulse, March 29, 2023, www.linkedin.com/pulse/breaking -down-one-medicals-results-how-branding-strategy/.

## CHAPTER 7

1.  Jeff Bezos, quoted in Jon Tan, "69 of the Best Jeff Bezos Quotes," Referral Candy (blog), September 18, 2019, www.referralcandy.com/blog/jeff -bezos-quotes.

2.  Neil Lindsay, quoted in Annie Palmer, "Amazon Cuts Hundreds of Jobs in Pharmacy, One Medical Units: Read the Memo," CNBC, February 6, 2024, www.cnbc.com/2024/02/06/amazon-cuts-hundreds-of-jobs-cut-in -pharmacy-one-medical-read-memo.html.

3.  Amazon, "Leadership Principles," About Amazon, www.aboutamazon .com/about-us/leadership-principles.

## CHAPTER 8

1.  Peter Drucker, quoted in Center for Responsible Business, "Peter Drucker on the Purpose of Business," Berkeley Haas (blog), February 9, 2016, haas.berkeley.edu/responsible-business/blog/posts/peter-drucker -on-the-purpose-of-business/.

2.  "State of Mobile 2013 (Infographic)," Super Monitoring (blog), Sep- tember 23, 2013, www.supermonitoring.com/blog/state-of-mobile-2013 -infographic/.

# ABOUT THE AUTHOR

Dr. Joseph Michelli is a certified customer experience consultant, a professor of service excellence, a professional speaker, and the chief experience officer of The Michelli Experience. He has authored *Wall Street Journal*, *Businessweek*, *USA Today*, and *New York Times* #1 best-selling books about his consulting clients, like Starbucks, Mercedes-Benz, the Ritz-Carlon Hotel Company, Zappos, and Airbnb.

Joseph transfers his knowledge of exceptional business practices through keynote speeches and workshops. These informative and entertaining presentations focus on the skills necessary to:

- Create memorable customer experiences
- Drive employee and customer engagement
- Enhance a commitment to service excellence
- Create quality improvement processes
- Increase employee morale

The Michelli Experience also offers guidance in:

- Customer and employee experience strategy
- Service excellence training
- Leadership team development services
- Group facilitation and team-building resources
- Customer and employee engagement measurement tools
- Customized management and frontline training programs

Dr. Michelli is eager to help you bring *All Business Is Personal* to life in your business. He can be reached through his website, josephmichelli.com, or by calling 727-289-1571.